THE NEW Machiavelli

THE ART OF POLITICS IN BUSINESS

ALISTAIR McALPINE

John Wiley & Sons, Inc.

New York ■ Chichester ■ Weinheim ■ Brisbane ■ Singapore ■ Toronto

Copyright © 2000 by Alistair McAlpine. All rights reserved.
Published by John Wiley & Sons, Inc.
Published simultaneously in Canada

This publication is designed to provide accurate and authoritative information in regard to the subject matter covered. It is sold with the understanding that the publisher is not engaged in rendering professional services. If professional advice or other expert assistance is required, the services of a competent professional person should be sought.

Library of Congress Cataloging-in-Publication Data:
McAlpine, Lord.
    The new Machiavelli: the art of politics in business / Alistair McAlpine.
        p.   cm.
    ISBN 0-471-29564-7 (cloth: alk. paper)
    ISBN 0-471-35095-8 (paper: alk. paper)
    1. Machiavelli, Niccolò, 1469–1527. 2. Management. I. Title.
    HD31.M3814   1998
    658—dc21   98-21069

Printed in the United States of America

10 9 8 7 6 5 4 3 2 1

To F.B. and D.B.
in recognition of their friendship
and help with this book.

CONTENTS

Contents

Contents

FOREWORD

Niccolò Machiavelli lived between 1469 and 1527. He resided in Florence where he practiced the art of politics — and to Machiavelli politics was truly an art, in the same way that carving a statue or decorating a ceiling was an art to his contemporaries. He held public office during one of the most exciting and turbulent periods of Florentine history. He also wrote a number of books whose reception was mixed, to say the least.

In one respect all of Machiavelli's early critics were agreed: this brilliant man surely went to hell. He is variously described as "an imp of Satan," as "hell born," as "a damnable fiend of the underworld," and as "the Great Master of Hell." In his excellent book, *Machiavelli, A Dissection*, Sydney Anglo points out that: "John Donne went so far as to describe a vision of the underworld in which Machiavelli, attempting to gain a place in Lucifer's innermost sanctum, was out-argued by Ignatius Loyola, founder of the Jesuits," and it was even possible for Samuel Butler to suggest facetiously that: "Old Nick himself took his name from Nick Machiavelli."

The greatest outrage was caused by Machiavelli's last and shortest work, *The Prince*, which was published after his death. Experts are at odds on the purpose of this book, some saying that it was written as an extended job application to impress the rulers of Florence, the Medici family, with Machiavelli's suitability for employment at their court. Certainly the dedication of *The Prince* to Lorenzo di Piero de' Medici was originally intended for his uncle, Guiliano, who died in 1516. The model used for the eponymous Prince is believed to be Cesare Borgia. Other contemporaries believed that the book was intended as a wicked joke, and that Machiavelli was giving the Medicis his advice in the hope that they would follow it and thus bring about their own downfall. In the event, Machiavelli failed either to get the job or to destroy the Medicis. He did, however, acquire a reputation for advocating a ruthless, scientific approach to politics which his contemporaries found abhorrent. It was the Romantics of the nineteenth century, such as Rousseau, who resurrected his writings. They argued that his works had a moral base: the belief that excesses of cruelty and dishonesty can be justified in the interests of patriotism.

Machiavelli's most enthusiastic admirers included Napoleon and Richelieu. Even the Marxists applied Machiavelli's methods, taking history as a guide to the future, just as Machiavelli is believed to have taken the actions of the ancients and used their examples to formulate strategies for his contemporaries.

Over the last twenty years I have read and reread *The Prince;* as a result, I have come firmly to the conclusion that Machiavelli was a brilliant student of human nature who, having observed how people were likely to act in specific circumstances, then justified his observations by quoting the actions of the ancients and certain contemporary princes as precedents.

There is no evidence to suggest that Machiavelli was himself an evil man. However, he clearly understood the capacity for evil that lurks in all of us. The point is not that Machiavelli advocated evil-doing; rather that he accepted that all human activity, and especially politics, will involve evil-doing. Having acknowledged that evil is unavoidable, Machiavelli tries to show his prince how to recognize it for what it is and how to use it to his own advantage.

In this book I have taken the lessons Machiavelli preached, added some insights gained in the course of my own perambulations through life, and applied them to the activity of conducting business. This is more appropriate than might at first seem to be the case, for, as will become clear, there is a striking similarity between the city states of fifteenth-century Italy and the great corporations of the last half of the twentieth century.

For reasons of continuity, I have changed the order of the chapters as they appear in *The Prince*. Into these arguments I have woven an apologue using characters who can be found in all businesses. The amiable employer, a person who longs to be liked; the able lieutenant, a person of honor and undoubted ability but with one failing—the fear of accepting ultimate responsibility; and the obliging employee, a person of some talent but with a distinctly limited ability, who is useful but is also cunning and greedy. These players illustrate the drama of a life in business, with all its attendant honor and dishonor, courage and cowardice, wisdom and folly: for each of us shares some of their characteristics and it is, as I shall demonstrate, circumstance that either brings them to the fore or keeps them in the background. The following pages, I believe, will help the reader find a safe pathway through the complicated world of business and equip him or her with the insights into human nature which are needed to survive in the jungle of greed and treachery that is commerce. Indeed, not only to survive, but to prosper, and to prosper with honor in what, when honorably conducted, is perhaps the most exciting and rewarding of all pursuits open to mankind.

Dedication: to His Magnificence Lorenzo de' Medici.

OF PATRONS AND PROTÉGÉS

Those men who are anxious to ingratiate themselves with a Prince are normally in the habit of greeting him either with those things they consider of the greatest value from amongst their own possessions or with objects they perceive give him the most pleasure. For this reason one often sees Princes presented with horses, weapons, gold-embroidered fabrics, precious stones and similar ornaments commensurate with their grandeur. Being eager, therefore, to offer my services to your Magnificence with some token of my subservience towards you, I have found nothing amongst my most precious and valued possessions of greater worth than my knowledge of the actions of great men, learned through extensive contact with contemporary events and a continual study of the ancients. Now that I have carefully considered and examined these matters at length, I have drawn them together in a small volume which I send to your Magnificence.

It is a common observation that business leaders seldom rise to their positions entirely through their own efforts; most will, at some stage, have benefited from the assistance of a patron. When speaking to such people they say, almost without exception, that there was one person without whose assistance they could not have achieved their success. Of course there are people who have succeeded without such assistance, but they are mostly found among those who inherit businesses and those who invent businesses, and they will be dealt with later in this work. For now, let us concentrate upon those who rise with the help of a patron and consider how they should set about finding a suitable patron and gaining his or her patronage.

Machiavelli, correctly, assumed that gifts will attract the attention of a patron; and the gift he offered was his own wisdom. This was probably a mistake—certainly, we should remember, Machiavelli did not get the job. A potential patron is not remotely interested in a protégé's wisdom—what a patron wants is an ornament to his or her court, a complement to the patron's own wisdom, not a competitor. This does not mean that the protégé should assume that a patron will accept shoddy gifts. On the contrary! What the patron requires are the time and the attention of protégés, who must, for the requisite period, give their souls to their patron. In return the patron will lift the protégé up life's great ladder, firmly placing the protégé's foot on each successive rung.

Machiavelli may also have made a mistake when he failed to "adorn my work with long phrases or high-sounding words, or any of those superficial attractions and ornaments with which many writers seek to embellish their material." The entreaties of a would-be protégé must always be prettily phrased: remember that flattery is a most valuable ingredient in the recipe for success, though only the protégé's strength of character can translate the recipe into reality. To quote Oscar Wilde: "Anyone who does not believe in flattery clearly has never been flattered."

In seeking a patron, the first thing a potential protégé must consider are the qualities of an ideal leader: not only will a good patron have these qualities, that patron will also look for them in anyone upon whom he or she intends to bestow patronage. A bad patron is of little use anyway and should be avoided, as such a person will only be looking for a follower who is willing to fetch and carry.

One must assume the ideal leader's normal behavior is guided by morality, for if you do not have a philosophy for life, how can you possibly have one for your conduct in business?

Loyalty is another important quality in a leader. To lead, one must have the ability to assess loyalty in those one leads, as well as an ability to demonstrate loyalty to those who follow. Such loyalty must not be a secret matter, but rather it must be demonstrated to all and sundry, in prosperity and adversity alike. It is essential to distinguish between those who are habitually disloyal and those whose disloyalty is pure opportunism; to be able to judge how deeply disloyalty lurks in their characters, and how carefully disguised it is. People who are capable of concealing their disloyalty are the most destructive people that a leader will ever meet.

Next, a leader must be trustworthy and what is more, be known to be trustworthy. Conversely, a leader cannot expect those that are led to give trust if the leader does not trust them.

Fairness is the next characteristic of a natural leader. One needs to be scrupulously fair, for a fair decision, even if it is disliked or even if it proves to have been wrong, will always command respect. If a leader criticizes, that criticism should always be objective, based on facts, not on hearsay reported by those with ambitions of their own.

The leader must also have the judgment required to assess accurately a follower's ability. Employees cannot be expected to inform their leader of the inadequacies that they try to hide, and the leader must never blame or penalize an employee for the leader's own misjudgment of that employee's ability.

A leader must always act in a way that commands respect, and beyond that, must always respect others, so that, seeing this, others will give respect in return. A leader must also demand respect at all times, and deal ruthlessly with those who do not show it—also those who use abusive language, disregard instructions with which they do not agree, and fail to cooperate with their colleagues.

A true leader will always resist the temptation to exchange old friends for new, no matter how attractive these new friendships may appear. One must never be persuaded by newcomers to follow a course against the advice of those who have always given their loyalty.

The leader must never shirk responsibility or fail to express gratitude and appreciation to others.

A leader must never be afraid to make unpopular decisions. One must always be one's own person.

Above all, any person who aspires to be a leader must look after their health, for without health a leader has nothing. Health is more than just the welfare of the body, it is the balance of the mind, the body and the spirit.

Finally, true leaders need a sense of history and an awareness of their own place in that history, for that is essential to their entire well-being.

It would seem that an aspiring leader demonstrating most, if not all, of the qualities I have described, would before long fall into the employ of a patron. This is not, however, normally the case. A person demonstrating these qualities is more likely to evoke the anger of colleagues than their praise. It is only the generous-spirited patron, or the opportunistic swindler, who will recognize the uses to which this person can be put. The first will seek to set that person's feet upon the path to fame and honor; the latter will try to make use of that person's qualities to deceive others.

Of course, most patrons do not live up to these ideals in every respect and the protégé should be aware of the pitfalls. All patrons require every ounce of their protégé's being: this will be confirmed by anyone who has held the position of protégé. But many patrons will try to suck a protégé dry and then cast that protégé aside. The wary protégé, being wise, knows this well and waits for the moment when such a patron can be discarded. Only in later years, when the protégé is established in the world of business, can that former protégé afford to acknowledge the debt and say, "I could not have achieved all this without the help of my patron." With the patron who has generosity of spirit and the protégé who has abnormal ability, matters are different. Here there is a true meeting of minds.

In adopting a protégé, the patron too takes risks. The potential leader may learn all the cunning of the servant and in this role break all of the principles that are the basis of leadership. Such a person may simply give up all aspirations to leadership and settle for the role of the permanent protégé, enjoying all the fruits of that role.

Ultimately, the true leader, having learned all that can be learned, breaks free. The patron of true generosity sets the protégé free. The one who would learn to lead must have the strength of mind to say "no" to the patron and to the easy circumstances which the patron offers. If the relationship is successful, there must be respect between patron and protégé. The patron must truly wish to help the protégé. The protégé must have courage, when circumstances demand it, to say, "a pox on your support."

In your search for a patron, first take a job that is lower than you believe you are suited to: patrons do not care for unemployed protégés. Demonstrate your efficiency at this job and you will rise and your reputation for efficiency will rise with you. Wave your reputation as a lure to passing patrons. Do not imagine that a patron will do your work for you. A patron will only help those already on the road to success. A patron can help the talented individual immensely, but a patron cannot make an ordinary person talented.

No ordinary person, however strong his patron, can become a leader. To obtain a position of leadership, and to lead successfully, requires a strength of purpose that only some humans are born with. This strength of purpose can be developed, indeed must be developed, but it cannot be acquired.

Anyone who aspires to lead others must take great trouble with their education. Read and listen all the time; but as for the formal education of schools, that is not necessary. Such education may help (and may also hinder). A leader needs the capacity for original thought, not just the ability to repeat the thoughts of others. Finally, not every potential patron has the qualities of a leader. Some are in a position to offer patronage simply as a result of chance. Though such people may be in a position to exercise influence on behalf of a protégé, they will not be able to offer what a protégé most needs—the opportunity to learn from a patron's example.

2

Concerning New Principalities Acquired by One's Own Forces and Personal Ability.

STARTING A BUSINESS

He should follow the example of the prudent archers who, when the target they want to hit seems too far away, bear in mind their bows' capability and set their aim considerably higher than the intended target, with the intention, not of shooting above it, but of reaching it with the help of the high trajectory.

These words of Machiavelli encapsulate the instincts of the one who would start a business. Always strive to achieve great things and then perhaps you will have a small success.

Wealth and position, both of which are constituents of power, are often believed to be the ambitions most likely to motivate men and women. It would, however, be a great mistake to believe that these are the only aspirations that cause individuals to break free from the normal pattern of their lives, or indeed to believe that the search for wealth and position are life's most efficacious motivating forces. This is far from being the case: jealousy is a far more powerful force than either of them. Jealousy is an oddity among forces, for the motivation of jealousy is irrational. Those motivated by jealousy do not need the evidence that they will succeed to embark on their project. Indeed, the practice of jealousy is self-destructive; but for all its self-destructive qualities, it is as likely to lead to apparent success as either the search for wealth or position.

The ownership of wealth automatically bestows position; position, on the other hand, is often achieved without wealth. Wealth may bring respect, but position can only be obtained from the respect of others, whether that respect be positive (admiration) or negative (fear). The quest for these qualities may provide motivation, but is not enough on its own to create a business empire.

First an aspiring proprietor must ask these questions: Why do I want to succeed? What do I regard as success? If the answer to these questions is that you require security and independence, then beware, for proprietors seldom enjoy security, and as for independence, the role of a proprietor must be entwined with the existence of the company. Without such an involvement, those who work for the company will not follow this new proprietor and will ask what is a leader's worth if that leader is not interested in the undertakings of that which the leader claims to lead? As Machiavelli puts it, "It facilitates matters when the Prince, having no other State, is compelled to reside there [in his new State] in person." Translated into business terms, this means that the new proprietor must be totally committed to the new company; for, as an agricultural expression has it, "There is no manure like the farmer's boot." In this total commitment to business, and one business in particular, there lies one danger: the new proprietor risks damaging both family and health.

The making of a business in the first instance comes from an idea—often a very simple idea such as that a group of people need a particular product. The idea is to fill that need. The idea need not be new; in fact, the idea on which a business, or for that matter, the philosophy of a life, is founded can be very old indeed. The genius of the person who starts a business is often to put an old idea in a new context.

So many who start their own business begin with a "good idea." Sometimes that good idea works, just occasionally that good idea will sustain a person in business throughout their entire career. More often than not that good idea will lead to bankruptcy—usually because of the cost of developing it. Machiavelli writes, "A wise man ought always to follow the paths beaten by great men, and to imitate those who have been supreme, so that if his ability does not equal theirs, at least it will savour of it." Here it is possible that the word "imitate" is wrongly used, for to imitate is the road to disaster, to emulate is the road to success.

Do not, however great the temptation, be an explorer or innovator with your new company. That route entails great costs and even greater risks. The returns from a company which is in advance of its time are small; the returns to a person in business who spots the good idea of another and develops it are often immense. Machiavelli writes, "And it ought to be remembered that there is nothing more difficult to take in hand, more perilous to conduct or more uncertain in its success, than to take the lead in the introduction of a new order of things. Because the innovator has for enemies all those who have done well under the old conditions and lukewarm defenders in those who may do well under the new. The coolness arises partly from fear of the opponents who have been on their side and partly from the incredulity of men, who do not believe in new things until they have had a long experience of them."

Not much has changed in five hundred years—the road of the innovator is still rough and uncertain. New proprietors who would also be innovators take the greatest of risks of all, for everyone's hand is turned against them. But the new proprietors who do take such a road and win despite its perils, are princes among pygmies who will strike them down.

I do not believe that the person who starts a great business empire necessarily has a dream; rather, that such people find that their original idea works on a small scale and then develop their idea along particular lines which continue to be successful when their business has grown into an empire.

The simpler the principles upon which a business is based, the more likely it is that they will be understood by those who work in that business, and thus the greater the chances of that business remaining successful. If the founders of businesses are able to pass on their ideas to their successors, then those businesses' prosperity will transcend generations. However, history shows that businesses passed from generation to generation will, in time, fail. This knowledge should be a terrible warning to those who inherit the power to run a business empire.

The founders of businesses must carefully study their own ideas, and, as time goes on and their businesses grow, present these ideas to their employees in such a way that their ideas become a creed. Here we must note the difference between the original idea, which is pure in the founder's mind, and the idea as seen later by the associates of the founder, by which time it becomes the perceived idea. Each new person who hears of the idea will adapt it to make it acceptable to their own personal standards.

There is, in this context, an essential difference between an idea and a dream. An idea has a universal application, while a dream is intensely personal and it confirms what you would like to happen rather than how you should make it happen. Nevertheless, an idea must incorporate elements of an intensely personal dream if it is to develop into the perceived idea which others can share, for the idea alone is a hard and rigid thing. Most humans, with all their failings, will grasp the idea only if its stark outlines are softened and will be encouraged to adopt it only if it appears to encapsulate elements of their own ideas. If they can be persuaded that the perceived idea is their own and not someone else's, then they will embrace it with enthusiasm.

In other words, the truly successful executive, whether that executive controls ten workers or one hundred thousand workers, will be something of an evangelist. The original idea, which was simply to profit from meeting a need in the community, must become a philosophy of how to provide that need; a concept that motivates both workforce and management. While its central idea remains strong, a business empire need fear no attack. Enemies will prowl around, even buy strategic stakes in the empire, but without success. Such businesses with an active idea as their focus are rare indeed, however their workforce will feel secure, and they will prosper.

Fairness must play a part in prosperity. Let the workforce own shares and take their share of the profits, for this will make the business both profitable and efficient. If there is no obvious way to improve a business, there is little point in a predator buying it or even the shareholders selling that business.

To those who have labored long in the service of others, the most tantalizing of prospects is that of owning a business. They see such an ambition as a race against age. However, they should not fear, for age is not the criterion of success; there is no merit in being young, nor disadvantage in old age. The factor that brings people to the point where they risk all to become their own master is simply courage, and it is fear which makes them hesitate.

Paradoxically, the more secure that an individual is, the greater that individual's need of courage. To risk nothing needs no courage at all; to risk much takes far more courage than it is possible to imagine. However, the courage to risk one's own future is not what I shall write about, this kind of courage is obvious to all. The courage that I am concerned with is the courage to take responsibility not just for your own future, but for the futures of those who will work for you. The courage to seize authority and with that authority to command.

The advice I have for the aspiring businessperson in this matter is that although such courage is God given, it is given to all of us. However, it is only a minority who choose to use it. To do so requires ambition. Courage is ambition carried through to success; ambition alone is merely dreaming and of little use to anyone. But it should not be thought that courage by itself will ensure success, though a lack of courage often brings failure.

The factor that counterbalances courage in business is fear. Fear is the safety factor, that feeling which the intelligent person in business gets, the tightening of the stomach, when buying a business or borrowing money. Fear is the feeling that people in business get in the dark hours of the night. Beware of fear in the night and beware, too, of ideas that come in the night and appear to dispel that fear. For darkness exaggerates the importance of both the dangers and the solutions. Under no circumstances should the businessperson engage in mental arithmetic after sunset. The dark hours should be used for sleeping, and if you must think, think of sex or food. For the plots and plans of the night are flawed, and what is more, the brain falsely stimulated forbids sleep. The ability to sleep soundly for a few hours and rise refreshed is one of the main ingredients of success.

The balance of courage and fear will change as circumstances change. The person with much to lose knows much fear. The person with nothing to lose cares little, if anything, for fear. Fear need not be purely a negative factor — fear can also be the spur to success. Fear and courage mixed together are the alchemy of success. In the end, money is not the spur to success. Talent is not a fire fueled by money. Talent is a red-hot furnace fueled by a passion to prove oneself a success; money is merely the measure of that success.

Starting a business is not an endeavor to be undertaken by straightforward people. The straightforward individual had far better find employment. Better that this individual prosper in the employ of a cunning master rather than seeking to employ others. The straightforward person accepts an order and carries it out as instructed. To the Machiavellian employer, this person has a quality beyond price. The straightforward person has no conceit and often a great deal of physical courage, which conflicts with their lack of confidence in their own ability to succeed. This person is often a leader, but seldom capable of building a business empire. Those who would start in business should seek out such a person, for they will make the perfect partner.

Among the first arts of business that you must learn is the art of saying "no." Say "no" with courtesy, but say "no" nevertheless. There is a balance that changes when a certain point is passed, when what seemed likely to be a good transaction becomes a bad transaction. It is often the case for those inexperienced in business to ignore that change or to imagine that such a change has not taken place for that is what they want to believe. In time, when these people consult the lawyers, as inevitably they will, the lawyers will say everything that they did was in order. They only made one mistake, they should not have signed the contract.

Never, in desperation, dupe another to seize an advantage in business. For those who are duped resent it terribly, and the short-term profit will bring you only long-term trouble. You do not need to stoop to chicanery in getting your business underway. You must have faith in your instincts, and time and circumstances will work in your favor.

The will to succeed must be strong inside everyone who would start a business, but it will not, by itself, be sufficient to gain success. Machiavelli writes, "It is necessary therefore, if we desire to discuss this matter thoroughly, to enquire whether these innovators can rely on themselves, or have to depend on others. That is to say, whether to concentrate their enterprises, have they to use prayers, or can they use force? In the first instance, they always succeed badly, and never compass anything; but when they can rely on themselves and use force, then they are rarely endangered. Hence it is that all armed prophets have conquered, and the unarmed ones have been destroyed."

And what are the armaments of business? The greatest of them is knowledge, coupled with the will and the ability to use that knowledge to your own advantage. But always remember that although know-how is useful when running a business, management is indispensable. Management is the foundation stone of all businesses.

The new proprietor should always remember that there is a great gulf between the role of the employee and the role of the proprietor. If the new proprietor has spent much time as an employee in the same trade that now constitutes the proprietor's business, it is hard to make the transition. It must be made, nevertheless, if the new proprietor is to succeed. The new proprietor must approach this new task with humility.

The new proprietor must put to one side the elegance and beauty of the ideas for creating a business, and devote time to the practical tasks of running a business. Those who would be a proprietor should first study bankruptcy. If you would like to know how a clock works, first take a clock apart. If you would like to know how a company works, first learn how to liquidate a company. In time, as you take over your competitors, this knowledge will prove invaluable. This knowledge will also prove indispensable in keeping your company clear of dire financial straits. All business is a risk and only fools believe otherwise.

The safest of transactions can become a liability by reason of war, or death, or earthquake, or strikes, or merely inclement weather. All transactions depend on timing, on each part falling into place: one default and all is in danger. The shrewd people of business plan for these disasters, the shrewd people of business assess the risks that they take and balance the extent of the risks against the value of their business.

When planning for the future, always take advice from someone who has failed rather than from someone who has known only success, for someone of intelligence who has failed will have contemplated that failure and determined the reasons behind it, whereas successful people often do not really know the truth of their success, only the myths that they have created for themselves. Machiavelli, in his time, was judged a failure.

A business started by one person will, in the beginning, be small. Small businesses often become isolated, focusing on what they produce. The new proprietors' time is largely spent dealing with the problems of their own businesses. Yet, those proprietors should be spending time looking at the products of competitors, studying the marketplace, studying the world situation, the markets in other countries, even though entering these markets is beyond their wildest dreams. The new proprietors must do this to be able to observe approaching storms which could tear their businesses apart.

Business is global in these days of easy communication and instant reaction, and realizing this, the new proprietor must be well-informed. For, to be well-informed greatly increases the chances of success. The fortune of the Rothschilds, it is said, was based on knowing the outcome of the Battle of Waterloo before their competitors.

The new proprietor, who is one deeply interested in making and selling products, must pay attention to the administration of the business. Administration cannot make a business, but the lack of administration will, without a doubt, ruin a business.

New proprietors are so often in a quandary, finding that their business cannot afford administrators. Administration is a trade, and the new proprietor must recognize it as such. The new proprietor must spend money on administration with the same enthusiasm that a new proprietor does not hesitate to spend money on premises. The new proprietor must study the figures that are produced to show the company's progress, but knowing about liquidation, the new proprietor must also see beyond the figures printed on the page. This is where real entrepreneurial talent is shown: where often the figures will spell disaster, the new proprietor may take a different view and with talent make a success of this business. These are the judgments that the new proprietor needs to make. This is where the new proprietor is helped by courage and saved by fear.

Financial controls, and the administrators who impose them, will often warn of financial danger: the new proprietor, however, often does not wish to be warned of risks. The new proprietor is busy in the act of manufacturing and selling the product, and responds to all warnings by trying to sell more and so to manufacture more. This is a fool's paradise, helping the cash flow but not addressing the fundamental problem that the goods being manufactured are more often than not sold at too small a price to bring stability to the business. All the while, business appears to be good, but the first downturn in the market will bring disaster.

The banks are no help, for they will lend when money is plentiful and business good and withdraw their lending when money is short. Do not imagine that because banks are willing to lend you money your business is sound, or for that matter, that because they refuse to lend you money, your business is unsound. Banks lend to sectors of business and when your sector is in favor, it is easy to borrow and likewise, when your sector is out of favor, the banks will not lend you a penny, regardless of the fact that your business is well managed. Only tight administration will tell you the truth about your financial situation.

All business is risky and the skill in business is to balance these risks, and as experience is gained, as the new proprietor becomes the old proprietor, you will almost instinctively avoid risks, and your friends and colleagues will start to tell you that you are too cautious. They will point out to you the great opportunities that you have missed and you, the old proprietor, will know that each of these opportunities was once a terrible risk, a risk in size disproportionate to your business. As time passes, if you are wise, you will expand your business, but only as time passes, for to expand too soon is often only a conceit, a self-aggrandizement.

The most dangerous characteristics found in those in business are vanity and conceit. Both of these vices destroy utterly, and bring down those who are close to the vain, and those around a proprietor who makes decisions based on conceit. For when the pursuit of money changes in you to the pursuit of prestige, you are in danger of losing both.

The first question to ask of expansion is whether you can afford to expand. The next, do you really need to expand, and finally, if you do expand, will you risk the whole of your business, or are you prepared to lose only that part of your business that you risk? Machiavelli points out that a number of historic figures have had fame thrust upon them, and concludes, "These opportunities therefore made these men fortunate, and their high ability enabled them to recognize the opportunity whereby their country was ennobled and made famous." In other words, they recognized success when they came across success. Machiavelli goes on, "Those men who by valorous ways became Princes, like these men acquire a principality with difficulty, but they keep it with ease." So it is with a business. Those who buy businesses with money easily earned, seldom keep them. Those who build businesses, usually hold them until in old age a different kind of proprietor takes over. Finally, there is but one test of success in business and that test is neither what others say of you, nor the figures on a sheet of paper—the important test is the amount of money in your bank account at each year's end. As for how you should treat your customers, it does not matter if you are starting a business or running an established business, whether your business is a one-person undertaking, or a vast organization—do not under any circumstances ever think evil of your customers, let alone speak evil of them. However dreadful a customer may be, or indeed how tiresome doing business with that customer may be, business is no place for the luxury of private feelings, and remember that however private your feelings, others will divine them, so learn to love that customer with a deep and enduring love, for without their custom you do not have a business.

3

Why The Kingdom of Darius, Conquered by Alexander, did not Rebel against his Successors after Alexander's Death.

BUSINESS AND GOVERNMENT

My answer to this problem is that all the principalities mentioned in past texts are found to be governed in one of two ways: either by a single Prince upon whom all the others are dependent and who, like ministers, help to govern that kingdom with his permission and favour alone, or by a Prince together with his nobles, who hold their position through their ancient lineage and not through the grace of the ruler.

However much the politicians of the right may wish to push back the frontiers of the state in its relationship with business, their efforts will be in vain. In Britain, where whole industries which were once controlled by the state have been sold to the private sector, the umbilical cord has, in reality, never been severed. Formerly, the state exercised its power over nationalized businesses by direction, and over private business by the threat of nationalization. Now the British state exercises exactly the same power by regulation, and

19

over those who run industry by the selective appointment to quangos and regulatory boards.

In terms of the freedom to decide its own fate, the latter state of business is considerably worse than the former. In France this has always been the case. Although business appears free, it is nevertheless shackled by the influence of the French government, which exercises control over large sectors either through the banks or through patronage. Even in America, where there is a culture of business independence from the state, restrictions are slowly throttling that independence, whether by legislation or through the courts awarding excessive damages to individuals who bring cases against corporations. In America, knowing the correct politician is as important a part of the strategy for running a business as all the other corporate paraphernalia. The large number of lobbyists in Washington is more than adequate evidence for this contention. The study of politicians and their habits is crucially important to any businessperson, for politicians advance or retard the cycles of opportunity which determine whether or not a business will prosper. A judgment must be made as to the way in which politicians are likely to behave because, in business, timing is everything. Business, like life, is about change and with change come chances which, once missed, may never be repeated. It is a tragedy if you fail to take advantage of such a chance because you cannot predict the behavior of politicians. You study politicians only to collect evidence that will enable you to predict the future actions of these people.

Never confuse power with influence. Always beware of the politician referred to as "powerful." Seek out the politicians who are referred to as "influential." Your world is the world of business and you must never succumb to the temptation to join the world of politics, for it will be your undoing. Concentrate on business and business alone, and you will succeed. However, always remember that politicians can affect your world without your knowing that this was their intention, unless you pay good heed to their world. For these worlds, so apparently disparate, are inextricably interlinked.

If politicians are indeed so important to business, how on earth can a thrusting young entrepreneur get to know them? The first rule is that politicians are not, in reality, hard to get to know. They are surprisingly accessible, for that is their trade—they must be all things to all people. Politicians are often careless in whom they know—not because they wish to be careless, for carelessness could seriously damage their careers, but because they have a natural inclination to see the best in those they meet, for they desperately need those they meet to see the best in them. When the relationship with a businessperson develops to a point where it is to the advantage of the politician, defects of character, obvious to almost everyone else, will be overlooked.

Politicians are, as a rule, deeply interested in politics, and given half a chance will turn any conversation to politics. The wise entrepreneur must learn much about politics in order to discourse freely and knowledgeably with politicians. The fact that an entrepreneur understands what politicians are talking about greatly flatters the politicians, and among all the range of people that you will meet in your business career, the politician is the one most open to flattery.

There must, however, be one word of warning here. Beware the politician of principle, for flattery, or the other inducements in the armor of the business, will only provoke that politician's hatred. The more you set out to seduce the politician of principle, the greater the enemy you will create. There is only one way to deal with a politician of principle. First, study this principled politician, listen to this politician's words as you would to any other politician. Probe to

21

find where his or her principles truly lie, for it is entirely possible that this politician, like so many others, has no real principles at all other than those of self-interest, conceit and political advantage.

The next step is to take time to discover what manner of person you are dealing with, for a mistaken judgment of a politician's character could bring about a dismal failure in your search for political influence. When you know the parameters of a politician's principles, that politician is yours for the taking, for as in the art of judo, you use your opponent's strength to your advantage. You simply apply the politician's principles to your problems and this principled politician has become your tool. The politician of principle is the finest tool you can find to help your business prosper—for that politician demands no reward, no entertainment, no favors in return. That politician operates on your behalf purely out of principle, and does not care who or what you are, where you come from, what you may have done or whether you are reputable or disreputable. What is more, a politician of principle is known to be honest and therefore that politician's words have the power of moral authority. Politicians of principle have a position in the parliament where they sit and they have the respect of their peers. However, politicians of principle usually have little or no direct power in the affairs of their party. These principled politicians are lonely figures who range around the edges of politics, uninterested in finding the right strings to pull. They are not silent or secret lobbyists. These principled politicians are the best allies in a pitched battle, for they are remorseless in the pursuit of truth and justice. Do not, however, use such a politician unless you intend to take a public stance and fight an issue until the end.

In practice, the entrepreneur who sets out to find political friends is most unlikely to come across politicians of principle—they are few and far between. Indeed, the entrepreneur is far more likely to meet the politicians who make a specialty of meeting entrepreneurs. They will welcome the entrepreneur and take him or her to parliament where they will introduce him or her to their friends and all of them will seek to impress the entrepreneur with the range of their influence. Such politicians are but the confidence tricksters who hang around the periphery of any society, and as a result, they are treated with contempt by those who have real influence. For those who have real influence do not spend that currency lightly. They are not easily approached, and neither are they for hire by the first person to pass by their office.

Why, you may well ask, do I not advise an entrepreneur to hire a lobbyist from the world of commerce? There are, after all, enough of such people who offer their services for money. The answer is simply this: it is not enough for an entrepreneur to lobby for his or her interests; an entrepreneur must do much more than that. The true student who wishes to rise in the world of business must learn to think like a politician. That student must learn the ways of politics and understand the forces that cause politicians to decide on their course of action. The person who would succeed in business must be competent in the art of predicting how a group of politicians will act, given a particular set of circumstances. That person must construct a business strategy taking into account a course of action of which the politicians have not yet thought. By acting in this way, the entrepreneur's company will prosper and the entrepreneur will be able to avoid the effects of a politician's actions that are so often harmful to industrial undertakings.

But how does a young person setting out in business acquire these skills? By reading or watching politics on television such a person will become informed as to what is happening, or rather what has happened. One must move in political circles to acquire political knowledge. Always remember this—either young or old—never, never, be ashamed to ask a question. Vanity is the downfall of mankind and the greatest vanity of all is to pretend understanding where no such understanding exists. Asking comes easily to youth, for youth is not expected to know and so no loss of face is experienced in not knowing. With age this is harder. You must, in order to succeed, swallow your pride and ask for enlightenment. Never neglect to ask and, if rebuffed, ask the same question of another.

To learn about politics, join a political party, for there you will meet those who talk of politics. Do not, however, fall into the trap of too great an involvement at any political level, for what you seek is not political power but a completely different commodity. You, the aspiring person of business, must acquire influence. Use political connections in order to meet politicians of all persuasions—and in parallel you will learn about humans, for politicians are humans, and politicians make up political parties, who in turn, form governments. Study how they behave and how they think, as you would study anthropology. Watch politicians carefully, listen to politicians intently, but never become party to their actions.

Despite being a member of a political party, keep yourself distant from the partisan aspect of politics, for in time you will need to discuss politics with politicians of all shades of opinion. Never, however, fear to be forthright in your political opinions, as those who remain neutral are but spectators and of little worth. Politicians do not naturally regard those with strong views that oppose their own as their enemies. Whether a person is your political enemy or not has much more to do with personality than politics. At this point, I must warn against people who would use politics to advance themselves for social aims. Such people are quasi-politicians and often quasi-business people, who never make much of a career in either field.

Sometimes the young person starting out in business may find it useful to establish a political organization, for to join an existing one and rise in its ranks takes time. This new organization is, in reality, little more than an excuse to call politicians together but it must have political credibility. The organization must never have the formality of membership, for members, in the end, demand a say in how the organization is run. Do not promise too much or deliver too little. Always remember you involve yourself in politics because you need the help of politicians, not because you wish to change the world.

Those who excel in business are totally unsuited to politics. In America, Ross Perot, a very able industrialist stood for the Presidency in 1992. Despite having the funds available to ensure success, he failed. The people did not trust him, and as a generality, the people do not trust those who are not politicians to take part in governments.

As I have written before, your knowledge of the politician's trade will become a passport to their world. Visit their world from time to time, be with them but never one of them. You are but a traveler in the business of collecting the evidence to take back to your world, which is the world of business. There is evidence enough to demonstrate how different these two worlds are — both business and the practice of politics are trades, but totally different trades. Business is like the game of billiards: you set up your shot having considered many possibilities. Politics is like tennis: you react and turn your opponent's shot against them. In business you are far less dependent on the skill, or lack of it, of your opponent.

Businesspeople who engage in politics understand that the only talent which politicians possess and which businesspeople lack, is the art of politics—an art which appears so simple, yet is so hard to practice. To succeed, businesspeople must stick to their own trade.

It is only when a businessperson has become truly cognizant of the ways in which politicians behave that it becomes apparent politicians in fact have very little power. Thus, at this juncture, it is important to speak briefly about another group within government, for within government the power lies for the most part in the hands of the civil servants. It is such people to whom Machiavelli refers in the quote used at the beginning of this chapter. Large businesses have no problem coming to terms with civil servants. Their fates are bound together. In office, the civil servants need the goodwill of the directors of large businesses, for once out of office and stripped of power, the civil servant will need a job. As retirement approaches, the civil servant will begin to think about the future and, filled with knowledge which might be of use to business, will approach the directors of large businesses with a friendly face, lunching and dining with them, paying great respect to their views. As for the person who runs a small business, one must catch civil servants early in their careers, spotting those civil servants who are likely to succeed and growing with them in all things.

Although such relationships may prove useful, the businessperson must remember that such activities are a great distraction from the main activity: running a business. Nonetheless, neither politicians nor civil servants can be ignored by those who would succeed.

4

On New Principalities Acquired with the Forces and Fortune of Others.

INHERITED BUSINESS

Those private citizens whom fortune alone makes Princes, become so with little effort but remain so only with the greatest of effort. They encounter no difficulties on their ascent—as they shoot to the top. All their difficulties begin once they have arrived.

It could be said that in this passage, Machiavelli refers to people in business who have only one idea, an idea so powerful that in time these people control vast businesses. The inventor of the idea has prospered, but cannot construct a business empire, for the inventor lacks both knowledge and courage, or has fear in too great a proportion to these. Being a victim of the fear of failure, the inventor will undoubtedly fail, and in the end others will run the inventor's business.

Another type of person in business is one who holds tightly to a company for fear that he or she could never start another. Furthermore, this person refuses to adapt the company to the practices of the age, clinging only to the one idea that brought initial success and rejecting all other ideas. In time, the person dies and the heirs sell the business, usually for a fraction of its value. An astute fellow businessperson may prey on such a business, not with the desire to own the idea or the business for its own sake, but rather for the capital lying idle in the business, as such companies accumulate cash with far greater ease than those that use their cash to research and develop new ideas, and have an ambition to grow.

There also exist those who inherit businesses. Providing that they have always worked in that business, then, at least in the short term, they should flourish. Machiavelli points out that those who take up residence in the states that they conquer hold them with far greater ease than those who reside elsewhere. On the matter of inheriting businesses, Machiavelli has useful words: "To stand simply upon the goodwill and the fortune of him who has elevated them, two most inconsistent and unstable things."

If, as so often happens, those who inherit a business know little of how to run that undertaking, they had best sell it as soon as possible. In circumstances where a quick sale is not a possibility, then Machiavelli again has some advice to those who "have not the knowledge requisite for their position." Machiavelli explains, "Unless they are men of great worth and ability, it is not reasonable to expect that they should know how to command, having always lived in a private condition . . ."; and continues, "Unless, as is said, those who unexpectedly become Princes are men of so much ability that they know they have to be prepared at once to hold that which fortune has thrown into their laps, and that those foundations others have laid before they became Princes, they must lay afterwards."

In short, those who inherit businesses of which they have little or no knowledge must learn *how* to run them *as* they run them. In truth, those who inherit businesses seldom succeed. Every year will bring new problems and the business must change or it will die. One of life's rarest qualities is the ability to change. So often, both in personal and business life, people continue to behave as though change has not happened, when it is obvious to all others that a change has occurred. The result of this is a slow decline towards disaster. Often people attempt to escape from the guilt of their own failure by manufacturing an intense dislike of others, usually of those to whom they are unable to fulfill their obligations. Facing up to the inevitable is perhaps the hardest task that a person engaging in business will need to overcome.

Timing is all in business, and if circumstances dictate that you must sell your business, do so *at once,* while you know the conditions that prevail. Do not take the risk of delaying the sale of a business that you cannot run, in the hope for better conditions; you may very well incur worse conditions, and you will almost certainly incur costs in waiting for that expected improvement in the market. You can only confidently make that choice between selling out quickly or waiting for the market to change when you have the financial or managerial strength that allows you to wait for good times. Without one or both of these, sell and sell quickly. Always remember that the cost of running down a company may well eat up the advantages of improving circumstances. These costs are always far larger than you would expect.

A business can never remain the same and the circumstances that dictate the profit or loss made by that business will never remain the same. Nor indeed do humans remain the same. If a business must be cut back, or reduced in size, this is only so that the business may one day expand. The perpetual small business does not exist. The whole idea of business is the manipulation of volatile masses: balancing them, putting them together and pulling them apart at exactly the right moment. Machiavelli describes how Alexander the Sixth, desiring the aggrandizement of his son, set about this task. The principles that Alexander used can be applied in a situation where a father buys a business for his son. "First he weakened the Orisini and Colonnesi parties in Rome, by gaining to himself all the adherents who were gentlemen, making them his gentlemen, giving them good pay and, according to their rank, honouring them with office and command." Here Machiavelli raises an important point. Never promote an employee above the employee's station in a newly acquired company, for it will only evoke the jealousy of other employees and they will set about destroying both you and the one you have promoted.

The new proprietor must be totally secure before deliberately upsetting the natural order of precedence in a company. The disruption that follows will certainly far outweigh the advantage of any reorganization. Machiavelli continues, "in such a way that in a few months all attachment to the factions was destroyed and turned entirely to the duke."

Machiavelli does have some words on promotion. He is against the promotion of anyone whom you have injured, or would have cause to fear you if they reached a position of power—"for men injure from fear or hatred." Machiavelli is not a great believer in the theory of a taste of carrot and a touch of stick. His preferred mode of action is to treat those who do not conform to their proprietor's will with a heavy touch of the axe. This method worked in fifteenth-century politics, for those touched with the axe could no longer complain. Today, the place of the axe must be taken by the deferred payment of compensation for loss of office. Never send an employee away so disgruntled that the employee has no alternative but to devote time and energy to your downfall. Always, always allow those whom you dismiss to go with honor, and always have regard for the bigger issues. Never create a situation where you spend more time dealing with a disgruntled ex-employee than dealing with schemes to make profit. Remember, it is almost inevitable that once you have removed one irritant, another will appear in its place.

Machiavelli, endlessly resourceful, has the solution in dealing with recalcitrant or truculent staff—you first hire another to do your dirty work for you. "There upon he promoted Romira d'Orco, a swift and cruel man to whom he gave the fullest power." This man, in a short time, restored peace. The Duke knew that it was not advisable to confer such excessive authority, for he had no doubt but that he would become odious, so he set up a Court of Judgement, in the country, under a most excellent president, wherein all cities had their representatives. He knew that the past severity had caused much resentment and hatred towards himself. He desired, in order to clear himself in the minds of the people and thus gain them entirely to himself, to show that any cruelty practiced had not originated with him, but with "The Minister." The estimable Romira, who had so speedily restored order to his master's estates, was taken one morning and murdered, and his body was left on the Piazza in Cesera, with the block and axe used in his demise beside it. Machiavelli wrote, "The barbarity of this spectacle caused the people to be at once satisfied and dismayed." This action was a masterly move, for it demonstrated both the power of the proprietor and removed the hated overseer at one stroke of the executioner's axe.

Clearly, it is not possible at the turn of the twentieth century to behead managing directors. Equally, at the turn of this century there is no need to take such extreme action, for a breed of men has risen to fill the role of the excellent Romira. It is possible to hire individuals who expect to work in a company only for a short period to fulfill their purpose: dismissing much loved employees; closing factories that are thought to be the life blood of the business; carrying out all manner of changes deemed necessary to make a business profitable, without blinking an eye or turning a hair at the horror of what they do. The proprietor can then dismiss these individuals when the proprietor judges the time to be right.

Both the proprietor and those who remain in the business celebrate the departure of the despots, and return to the job of running a business recently cleansed of the impediments of waste and habit. The individuals who perform this useful function take all the blame for the unpleasantness that they have caused with them, and they are happy to do so for the amount of the blame that they carry is their recommendation for their next job.

Alexander had, according to Machiavelli, carried out all the actions necessary to place his son in a position of power. Alexander made only one mistake: he died; and all came to nothing—the Grand Plan came unstitched. No matter how brilliant the aspiring businesspeople may be—all is worthless unless they take care of their health. Without health they will create nothing and pass nothing on to their families. Finally, for those who would acquire companies, either by inheritance or good fortune, it is important first to do your homework, work out a plan and carry that plan out ruthlessly if need be, or kindly if that way is more propitious to its conclusion. Do not hesitate for any reason and do not under any circumstance delay, for in delay all can be lost. Remember also that all people are mortal, and likely to die unexpectedly. You should make plans for such a turn of events. Prepare your successor, for your successor is not a competitor, rather a form of life insurance. There is no point in appointing a successor who is a weak person, for such an action is pure vanity. The successor cannot be a patient person, for patient people are seldom full of ideas. So your successor's patience must be rewarded and the successor must know what that reward is to be and what his or her duty is and, as patience is not part of the successor's character and it is likely that impatience is, the successor must know that it is worthwhile to control that impatience. Should you suspect that there is a move afoot to hasten your departure, advertise for a successor despite the fact that you do not need or indeed want one. In this way, you discover who it is in your company that wants your job and is causing all this impatience. There can be no confusion if this strategy of selecting your own successor and of leaving in your own time is to flourish. Sadly, few who succeed in business either go when they want to, or are succeeded by the one that they prefer.

5

On Hereditary Principalities.

FAMILY BUSINESS

I hold, therefore, that with states that are hereditary and accustomed to the blood-line of their Prince there is less difficulty in holding on to them than with new ones, since it is sufficient to leave the pre-existing order established by their ancestors undisturbed, and only make alterations as circumstances dictate. In this way a Prince who is of average capability will always keep his state unless an extraordinary and excessive force deprives him of it.

In business, as in the rest of life, princes of average ability become even more average with each succeeding generation, and it is the job of a prince (or employer) to spot the advent of "extraordinary and excessive forces." Princes of average ability fail to spot disaster as it approaches, in the same way that they fail to spot opportunity.

Of the various activities undertaken by mankind, be they in business, politics or sport, the most hazardous of all is conducting your life in the midst of your family. While there is much that you can achieve, there are few, if any, ways of controlling your destiny, as you must become subservient to the group. In a family, free will does not exist, nor can free will exist and the family remain intact.

In a successful business of any kind there is one ingredient which is vitally important, and that is discipline. In a

35

family business, discipline is almost always missing. A family business works on a territorial system evolved over the generations with each member of the family having specific responsibilities and usually guarding these responsibilities fiercely. Open criticism is muted for there is a limit to how rude you can be to a family member, while privately these criticisms flourish.

There are two kinds of family businesses. The first is a business controlled by members of the same family for more than one generation, and run for the benefit of themselves and perhaps even the wider members of their family. The second is a business controlled by one person, who intends to pass on the control of that business, usually to a son or sons, exceptionally to a daughter.

Once a business has belonged to two generations it is usually on a sound financial footing. If the third generation does not, in the words of Machiavelli, "Transgress Ancestral Images," that generation will remain secure. There is, however, another precept far older than Machiavelli's words and that says, "From cobbler to cobbler in three generations," for unbelievably, it is success that kills the family business. The more successful each generation is, the less likely that each generation which follows will either want to work or, indeed, need to work. The family which will survive must want to survive, want to work and be prepared to make the sacrifices necessary to survive. If a family business is run efficiently, that business does not need rules because those who manage are ever present to divert, guide and to reward. These active and able members of a family will make the rules as they go along, changing them to suit the business climate.

If failure looms, a family may be tempted to introduce new blood, and find a man or woman who they believe is talented enough to run their business for them—this could well be their downfall. At best, their business will be stolen, and at worst, destroyed. However friendly such a person may seem when first employed, however much that person may declare that it is their intention to turn the business around for the benefit of the family, given the power to control, that person will turn that business around only for their own prestige and profit. The newcomer will suggest economies to the family and arrange share options for him- or herself. The trappings of power enjoyed by the family will be stripped from them in the name of economy, and handed to the newcomer in the name of necessity. For a time, the business may prosper but it will no longer be a family business, for there will be new shareholders introduced with new money and there will be new directors— great men and women from the boards of other companies, and their one qualification will be that they know little or nothing of how to run such a company on whose board they now sit. In time, they may even replace the newcomer, for as Machiavelli wrote, "One change always leaves the way prepared for the introduction of another." Machiavelli continued, "And if he [the Prince or employer] should be so deprived of it [his business] whenever anything similar happens to the usurper, he will regain it." This is untrue, for average princes seldom recover the businesses founded by their families, except perhaps as figureheads working for the future owners of those businesses, nor do they find it easy to gain employment elsewhere. Families should therefore beware of losing the business, for to lose a family business is to lose all.

The threat of failure should spur the controlling members of a family business into action. They must seize on the possibility of failure to introduce reforms. Families, by their very nature, span the generations, so they are reluctant to consider dramatic reform unless the circumstances are dire. This feature is both an advantage and a failing—for in successful families reforms happen slowly as the power of one generation fails, and the power of the next increases, and the family "never transgresses the customs of their ancestors." Employees of these companies will respect such slow reforms and these companies will prosper through those generations. As Machiavelli wrote, such princes will always be of "ordinary assiduity" and will always be able to maintain their position by adapting to unforeseen circumstances, unless some very exceptional force deprives them of those positions, which, of course, it will in the end. In successful families, reforms never happen, for one generation merely copies the conceits and the errors of the last.

Those who run family businesses must, however, take into account the vagaries of governments and the either malicious or ignorant politicians who often control their actions. Politics will often have a disproportionate effect on a family business. The family that realizes its business is approaching trouble, and sees that reform is necessary, must take a courageous course and commit themselves to making reforms at once. These reforms will probably not be welcomed by most of their employees, but the threat of failure is enough to convince those that grumble of the need for reform to save both the company and their jobs. Machiavelli points out that time heals such grievances and that over a long period the memories and causes of innovation will be forgotten. Often the drawback to a family taking action to save its business is that those not engaged in the business prefer to sell rather than to take the risks of reforming and regenerating the business. For inasmuch as a family strengthens the respect that the members have for one another, it also strengthens the contempt that they have for each other when that respect dies, killed by failure.

The second type of family business—the would-be family business—is a much less certain affair. If the founders of such a business are dramatically successful, their heirs will have no interest in the running of the businesses that they inherit, and they may indeed have no inclination to work at all. The founders often set up complicated trusts and write complex clauses into their wills—they are determined to pass on their life's triumph, the business they have created. Their heirs, however, may see this triumph as an impediment to their lives—that they must inherit a business instead of money. Such a business ends in the hands of the lawyers who sell it or run it, usually rather badly, and supposedly for the benefit of the family members whose trusts these lawyers control. Far better that they sell the business than run it to suit their own ends and so ruin that business. For a family business to succeed, not only must the founder have succeeded, but the business must be left to the heirs in a manner where all depends on the continuing success of that business. The founder's relatives must be brought into the business at an early age and taught early that the business's success is reliant upon those who work in it and directly related to how hard they work. They must show respect to gain respect, express gratitude and appreciation of others, and take firm and often unpopular decisions. They must learn to lead, and learn that they must often take the blame for the follies of others. If they do not understand these things, then they will fail and their inheritance will be stripped from them, for bankruptcy is the spur to capitalism.

❊   ❊   ❊

Having briefly described some of the pitfalls of a family running a business, I shall write of how to take a business from a
family, for if a predator will capture a business, that predator
must first know the habits and inclinations of those who own
and run that business. Families running their own businesses
have one great weakness, and that is conceit. These proprietors live in a world of their own. A world where no one can
say "no" to them—in the final analysis those who run family
businesses know that their word cannot be gainsaid. They
have in their minds either the conceit of rejecting the views of
others, or the conceit of hearing no other views except those
that they believe to be wrong and that they have no need to
accept. This conceit must be used to seduce the family who
work in the business that you seek to capture. Offer them a
better position in the joint corporation, better only because
the business will be bigger; offer some of them the chance to
do something away from the business; offer the person raised
in a family business escape; offer those mesmerized by their
family businesses security of tenure and less hard work; offer
the members of the family who own shares, but do not work
in the business, money; offer to make the name of the family
famous. Tell them what they do is honorable, for all people
like to receive money in order to be honorable. Speak of the
future and the workforce—never speak of need, failure, necessity, nor adverse circumstances. Never appear to be doing
the family a favor—rather make it appear to them that they
do you a favor. Promise faithfully never to dismiss loyal servants, and talk of sports fields and staff facilities and naming
them after the family. Talk of the great things that "we" can do
together and, above all, offer them profit. For these are the
weasel ways that will separate a family from its birthright.

Always remember that if you are under attack by a foe
who would take your business, timing is of the utmost im-

portance and in good circumstances there is no enemy as remorseless as time. However, in adverse circumstances there is no ally as helpful. Evil events, as with good events, take far longer to come to fruition than it is possible to predict. Under attack and without hope, always seek refuge in the great uncertainties of life. What will happen in the future or indeed what the outcome of a legal action will be, no one really knows for certain.

6

The Classification of Principalities and How they are Acquired.

CAPTURING A COMPANY

All the states and all the governments that have had, and have, power over men have been, and are, either republics or principalities. Principalities are either hereditary, in which case the blood-line of the Prince has been long established as ruler, or they are new. These new principalities in turn are either brand new, as was Milan to Francesco Sforza, or they are like limbs joined to the hereditary state of the Prince who acquires them, as is the Kingdom of Naples to the King of Spain. The dominions acquired in this way are either used to living under a Prince or accustomed to being free; are either acquired with the arms of others or with the Prince's own, and either acquired through the agency of fortune or on account of personal strength and ability.

The number of systems by which businesses are controlled are far less than might be expected, and it is necessary to understand each of these systems if you are to capture a business that operates by one of them.

In terms of success, the strongest of these systems are the businesses owned by trustees. This type of business, if sound, is almost impossible to conquer—however, under the threat of failure, these businesses are the easiest to over-

43

come. The risks taken in trying to acquire a successful business controlled by trustees either by friendly means or force, are immense. However, so are the rewards that flow from successfully conquering such businesses.

Trustees are almost always without the requisite talents needed to act as proprietors. They are not required to produce maximum profitability, only to run a business prudently—a word which covers a multitude of sins. Often they allow the businesses in their charge to deteriorate, seldom using the company's funds efficiently, often allowing them to accumulate; leaving a pot of gold to tempt the predator. Trustees must do this, for their first thoughts are for their own protection. In bad times, when a pot of gold must be spent, trustees are without defense and they wish to rid themselves of their obligations, the running of the business having become tedious. The lack of profit takes away both the personal comforts that flow from their positions and the prestige of running the business. Trustees, finding themselves with a failing business and increasing responsibilities, usually decide to sell. However, when times are good, trustees will often acquire other businesses that neither they nor their staff know how to run. Seldom are these trustees concerned to achieve maximum profitability from newly acquired subsidiary companies, for to do this only causes ill will and trustees avoid ill will like the plague. Again, such actions by trustees create more prizes to be won by the predator.

Take note, however, that while trustees may well be lacking in their talent for management, they excel in their talent for preserving their jobs and the style of life that attends on those jobs. Prestige and conceit are both their strength and their greatest weakness. Those who are practiced in the art of acquiring businesses are attuned by instinct to these weaknesses and acutely aware of the trustees' vanity and pride.

There cannot be too strong a warning given to those who would engage in a conflict with trustees. For although they may be unfit to run a company both by training and character, trustees operate from the position of not having to produce results. Profit is not their function, and trustees by their very nature are risk adverse. They have had both the time and funds to devote to patronage and undoubtedly will have many friends in powerful positions who would wish these trustees to remain in control of the business. Beneficiaries are without any power while business is good and, when business becomes bad, then beneficiaries begin to have influence but still no power.

The best approach to negotiate with trustees is through flattery. The trustees, first and foremost, are interested in the price to be paid to them, in personal contracts and in perks. Second, they are concerned with what other people will say. They must appear, at least, to have negotiated the best deal — flatter them and allow them to appear to win. Often they care little about the reality of victory, only apparent success — a success that is in truth a failure, the result of their own greed.

When negotiating, always remember never to attribute your own instincts and emotions to others, for trustees with whom you negotiate will not behave as you would behave. Listen very carefully to the words that *people do not say,* for it is often in the words that they hide, that the truth lies. Remember also that indifference is one of the most powerful tools during any negotiation. A person who does not care deeply about anything can negotiate brilliantly. The reverse is also true, if you care too deeply, that care inhibits your ability to negotiate. Always be well-informed about the company that you wish to acquire — know about its industry and the countries where it operates. To be well-informed is to be wise.

Ask yourself frequently, "Why do I need this business?" And if at any time the answer is because of position, conceit or self-promotion, walk away. The true answer to this question must be, "The acquisition of this company fits neatly into my plans and will increase my profits, while at the same time cutting my costs." Always be prepared to walk away from a deal—there is only one purpose in negotiation and that is to acquire the company at the right price.

The most common variety of business is one with disparate shareholders, with some shares being held by its founder or the founder's family, some by institutions, perhaps banks and financiers who finance the undertaking, and others held by investment trusts and pension funds. Some shareholders may even have no interest in the company other than a belief that its shares will increase in value. These companies are the most vulnerable to takeover. This may be the weakest structure of a company, but only if there is an apparent weakness in the skills and ability of the management, a weakness that the predator will be able to remedy, or if there is a marriage value—a merging of companies that will reduce the overheads of both companies and increase the overall profits.

The takeover is distinctly Anglo-Saxon—the market economy works at its best in Anglo-Saxon countries, allowing the takeover to flourish. These days there are takeovers in almost all countries, however America is probably the most proficient. Britain, after America, has the most sophisticated machinery for takeovers. At the other end of the scale is Russia and somewhere in-between are Germany, France and Spain.

Takeovers can be friendly or hostile—they seldom, however, happen without hostility. When friendly takeovers occur, they are called mergers—a neat word that disguises the intent of the staff who control the stronger partner to use their strength in disposing of the staff who work for the weaker partner. If the word massacre were used at the outset, without doubt many of these uncontested takeovers would not take place.

Be assured, mergers are savage operations. The results for the management of the smaller partner is much the same as in a hostile takeover. Due to the infighting and jockeying for position after a merger, the time scale of a director's destruction is more extended, and perhaps the director's remaining without power or going with reward is more elegantly conducted than would be the case after a hostile bid has succeeded.

In the City of London hostile takeovers have taken place on an average of one a week since the end of the war. In Frankfurt only four such bids have taken place in the same time frame. In other countries, such as Germany and France, it is the rigidity of a state-controlled economy that prevents the predator entrepreneur from being able to maneuver. In other countries, businesses change hands with the help of banks, pension funds, and even governments.

Governments should stay far from industry—neither hindering its function with their regulations, nor pretending to help its function with the taxpayers' funds. In fact, for a government to save a company from bankruptcy is worse than for a government to consign a company to bankruptcy, for bankruptcy is the spur to capitalism and its point must never be turned or blunted by the actions of politicians. Bankruptcies, like the recession that so often causes them, are a necessary function of the free market.

With a hostile takeover, only price matters, and the highest price wins the prize. The return on capital is all. The conglomerates taking over a company may sell part of it at once and keep another part for fattening, for sale at a later date. Often the industrialists who run these conglomerates will never meet those who work for them—they fear that a personal liking for an employee may stay their hand when a disposal has to be made. The predators justify their actions thus: they take companies that are badly run, they improve them, break them up and place them in the hands of people who can run them, often by selling them to the employees. Strangely, the public do not see these people in this light. More often than not they are seen as undertakers, those who bury a company, rather than save it.

There is, in truth, no moral justification for savage behavior in life or in business, and those who practice it are destined for obscurity or are remembered only for their brutality. One of the great ironies of life is that those who fight hard, but with an alert social conscience, find they are only remembered in proportion to the flamboyant generosity of their monetary donations, by having their names attached to the wards of hospitals or to annual prizes and lectures. Seldom, if ever, are they remembered for how they made this money.

Remember, when you would take over another company and play the exciting game that is business, however attractive a situation may look when you set out to buy a business, ask these questions, "Where is the exit point? How can I sell the business that I intend to buy? Where and when will I see a return on my investment and my capital back in my bank account?"

7

On Mixed Principalities.

CONTROLLING A CAPTURED COMPANY

Consequently all those who have been injured in occupying that principality are enemies.

This is an important warning for those who take over companies. The aim of the takeover is to make the victim company more valuable, and this added value cannot be achieved if the employees of your new acquisition are your enemies. After savage action for reform of the new acquisition is implemented, it is imperative that the dignity of those who remain be assured.

Machiavelli's words of advice for those who conquer and rule countries are as relevant for those who would conquer and rule companies. He quite rightly points out that people change masters willingly—hoping to better themselves—however, they are seldom satisfied in that aim. Takeovers are not kind affairs, usually ending in reorganization and redundancy in order to make the company more efficient. As Machiavelli wrote, "You cannot maintain the friendship of those who have helped you obtain this possession." Agreements made during takeover are seldom honored in their original spirit. The friendships that were essential in the battle may now be seen as impediments to the future, facts that were overlooked are now believed to have been hidden and plans for a glorious future talked of during the battle are shelved. Suddenly, the proprietors and their staff who were so helpful are now distasteful to their new masters.

Both the employees and employer who prospered under private ownership find the cultural change to a corporate venture distasteful to them and what is more, often these people who were perfectly suited to their former private state cannot make the change to their new corporate state. The decision making and collective thinking of a group is dramatically different from that of a private or small company. The cultural change from individual to collective thinking is too great for those in senior positions to survive and still to be effective. As a result, they fail in their duties, are dispensed with and become just another economy, sacrificed to the efficiency of the new corporate empire of which their former company is now a part.

When an entrepreneur sells to such a group, whatever is agreed or promised, it is far better that the entrepreneur goes. One creative person does not take over from another. A creative person starts a business of their own, a group prospers by being efficient and disciplined. The two most important elements of a group are administration and financial control, after these comes imagination, which for the individual came first. However, the implementation of a person's imagination is seldom either cost effective or efficient, only financial control and efficient administration ensure that individual's success. In time, however, that individual becomes tired and loses the way, then the individual or the institutional shareholders sell that business. When a group reaches its maximum efficiency, that is the time when there is again a need for entrepreneurial talent. A talent that was so easily dispensed with when the group bought the entrepreneur's business is now a very hard talent to find. Corporate managers do not take risks, entrepreneurs do take risks. Those with ideas often cannot focus on accounts, while those who understand accounts can seldom produce ideas. The entrepreneur, unlike the accountant, understands that what you see on paper is not necessarily the full picture. Among all the change a takeover causes, many who work in the business will go. It is true that in the aftermath of a takeover some of the old order will stay, but they will stay without power. A few of these who remain may, in time, even rise to positions of influence, but seldom to positions of real power.

Now is the time to quote what surely must be Machiavelli's most famous precept: "Men must either be caressed or annihilated, they will revenge themselves of small injuries but cannot do so for great ones; the injury therefore that we do to a man must be such that we need not fear his vengeance." It is most important for the new owners who would control and operate profitably their new company that, in Machiavelli's words, "the family of the Princes which formerly governed them, be extinct."

Machiavelli lived in the days of the knife that came in the night, or poison delivered with the breakfast—ours is an age which demands subtler methods. The most subtle, and by far the most effective way to deal with former directors is by promotion, not just in position, but in lifestyle: a new house with a large garden to occupy the mind, a tiring tour visiting the company's subsidiaries around the world—the pace must be fast and the tour long. A company car should also be provided and on top of this a massive amount of work should be given to the promoted director, not making decisions but writing and reading reports. Let these directors who are impediments to the future wither on the vine. However, do not dramatically change the work practices of the employees of the new company. As far as possible let them lead their lives as before. If economies must be made, and it seems that new management will always find scope for economies, then sell a division, or close a whole department, but never tinker with companies. Always massage the morale of a company that you have taken over. If you are the predator and are victorious, move your office into the victim's building, making yourself available to the staff of your new company. Your presence will give them great courage, for a business that is supervised will always prosper but one that is neglected and left in the hands of others will falter.

As the new employer remakes the company, possibly the most important task will be the restructuring of the group's debt. As a result of this acquisition, the new debt that has been taken on must be dealt with. To neglect this debt and imagine that inflation or profits will deal with it, or to allow other acquisitions to mask that debt, always rolling the debt forward as your company appears to grow, is the utmost folly. Debt must be considered in an orderly fashion and dealt with in such a way that your resources are not fully stretched.

In dealing with debt and the restructuring of a business's finances, a military concept is useful. Imagine a formation of troops advancing across a field of battle in an orderly fashion. Some will fall as the advance proceeds, but in their place will march other soldiers held nearby for that purpose. Each part of your army that is debt will be supported by other parts of that army. The destruction of one part must never be allowed to affect the strength of the whole. Always remember that a group of companies is as strong as its weakest link.

Do not waste the time of your top people running this new acquisition. If they become bogged down with a particular company, the profits from future ventures will evaporate. Instead, move your middle management into positions of influence and use them to infiltrate your new possession and use your new situation as a vehicle to locate other companies to buy and so make this new company even larger. Always consider the prospect of selling the company that you have bought to those who run that company, let them believe that this is to be their company in the end. Being close at hand, you will be able to assess the mood of those who work there and observe how efficient are those whom you have sent to work there. If the inconvenience of having to change the location of your place of work worries you, then perhaps you should consider whether you are dedicated to the activities in which you are engaged, whether the running of companies and the improving of their fortunes is really how you wish to spend your time. Having captured a company, the wise employer must now change character. Where once the employer was savage, the employer is now methodical. No longer a predator, the new employer must remake that company with the skill of a surgeon. The new employer in this task demonstrates one of mankind's strongest instincts—the desire to improve. Employees sensing this desire will be drawn by the power of that instinct and join in this activity. The art of the takeover is a fine one, worthy of the title, "Art."

Those who excel in this art are indeed true artists in the fullest sense of that word, for, at their best, they demonstrate a creativity and originality of thought seldom found among those who merely engage in business. Consider first the balance that must be kept by the predator—a balance between looking far ahead for more victims and watching behind lest a greater predator takes you as a victim.

Finally, Machiavelli has wise words for those who have treacherously assisted in the takeover of the private businesses for which they work, hoping no doubt to win favor from those who are the new masters. "From this a general rule is drawn which never, or rarely, fails: that he who is the cause of another becoming powerful is ruined: because that predominance has been brought about either by astuteness; or else by force, and both are distrusted by him who has been raised to power."

In the coming pages, I will construct an apologue describing three different characters—the obliging employee, the able lieutenant and the amiable employer. It is true that most employers are far from amiable; however, the term "amiable" suits my purpose, for it encapsulates the characteristics of such people who fail in business. They are often careless, lazy, idle in the matter of detail and, above all, for a time lucky and so able to be amiable, for in business, as in life, to be kind is the greatest of luxuries. I shall proceed with the precepts of Machiavelli, endeavoring to show that there is a deeper truth in the ways that humans behave. It is a truth that all of us would rather hide.

8

How Cities and Principalities, which Prior to Occupation were Accustomed to Living under their Own Laws, Should be Administered.

THE RUNNING OF A RECENTLY ACQUIRED BUSINESS

There are three ways of holding on to those states that one acquires which are used to living freely and under their own laws. The first way is to destroy them. The second is to go and live there oneself. The third way is to let them continue living under their own laws whilst levying a tribute and ensuring they remain your allies by creating a well-disposed ruling élite.

Machiavelli's choices of the ways to deal with a recently acquired state are very similar to the choices available to one who has recently acquired a company. To run a recently acquired company is no easy matter and when that company has been accustomed to a willful management, it can be extremely difficult to impose your own ideas on the existing management.

Possibly the most important aspect of business, as of life, is knowing exactly what you want. First, consider why you have acquired this company. Its activities may blend with the activities of your own company, or maybe it is that your own company needs to diversify its activities. Change is the nature of business and, this being so, the company that has one product or operates in one field is in considerable jeopardy. Change can also be forced on companies by a wide variety of other factors: trends—your product may go out of fashion; technology—your product may become redundant, as the importing of ice from Iceland was made redundant by the invention of the refrigerator; regulation—your product may become too expensive to manufacture due to regulations introduced by government. Society may even turn against your product, as it has recently turned against smoking cigarettes, certain perfumes and even the eating of fatty foods. Your mind must always be alert to change and the only way that this can be so is for you to be well-informed. Many people can predict change, but few can bring themselves to make dramatic changes when these changes are necessary.

It is possible that you have made this acquisition purely to expand the size of your company. There can also be technical reasons for this acquisition—the company has a product or an executive that you require. Sometimes a company is acquired purely for the value of its assets, the staff are dismissed and the assets are sold. Even conceit is a reason for a purchase and this is the reason more often than most people imagine.

Once the true reason for the acquisition of an existing company is clear in the mind of the purchaser, the purchaser can then decide on the course of action that needs to be taken. The first of Machiavelli's three choices on how to deal with the companies that are taken over is to ruin them.

I interpret this course to mean the liquidation of the company recently acquired and the sale of its assets.

Some predators will set out to sell parts of the company to those who work there. This is convenient, but far from the most profitable course of action. No one knows more about the value of a company than those who are intimately involved in the running of that company, and no proprietor, nor shareholder, nor lawyer, nor banker has a greater knowledge of how that business functions, and what its parts are worth, than have the very people to whom you are trying to sell a part of the business. Rest assured, they will buy only the best parts at the poorest price. The alternative is to seek purchasers for the active business in the marketplace: a very hazardous undertaking. The management that you have recently acquired, knowing that you have no confidence in them, will, in all probability, leave at a time far from convenient to you. Therefore, it is necessary to take a holding position, and convince the management of the company that they are indispensable. Coax them, cajole them, use whatever means are needed to persuade them to stay until they are no longer needed. Unless the value of a company's fixed assets far exceeds the price that you have paid, do not embark on the course of ruining a business.

Machiavelli states the next choice available is "to reside there in person." This is interpreted to mean that you should run the company yourself. If this course of action is to be taken, let us consider why the company came on the market in the first place: for any company to be acquired by another must mean that the company is flawed. The fact that the company has been acquired—whether by a takeover battle, the death of a major shareholder or any other of a dozen reasons—demonstrates that the company could not, in reality, have continued unchanged on its own.

Even if the acquisition is called a merger and conducted on friendly terms, do not be misled. It is far better that those who run that company leave the company and engage in a pursuit where their talents will find endless challenges and no one will challenge their style of decision making. The chances are that entrepreneurs who have made the decision to sell have become scared of taking risks. Where possible, dismiss these people with honor, whatever their reputation. Reputations are about the past, business is about the future.

There are two types of people in business who would be wealthy. The first is the one who makes a single coup. Such a one takes a company and builds it. When, having built the company, this person attempts to run it, it will inevitably not be a success. The entrepreneur then sells or is forced out, for those who make one coup seldom make another. The second type of wealthy person is the person of ideas and I will write of this type of person later.

. When one business is acquired by another, in order to form a larger business or a group, the day of the sole proprietor is gone. For when the sole proprietor becomes the colleague of another, or indeed several others, the new situation will be intolerable for all of them. The sole proprietor's instincts are totally against consulting with others and such a person's greatest talent lies in being able to think and to decide as an individual. The imaginative qualities of a group are rarely as effective as those of one person, but that group makes up for this loss of effectiveness with a considerable increase in efficiency. As a company grows by acquisition, so the culture of that company changes and it depends on more efficient management. The days when the company was run by flair and imagination have given way to financial controls.

If indeed the company that you acquire is already run by a group of people and the flaw in that company is one where the group has run out of energy, or become lazy, that is when they in their turn need the talents of one person, for these people have reached their point of maximum efficiency. At first they manage the business better than its previous owner, but the cultural change that they introduced can never be permanent, and the time has come for that culture of management and financial control to adapt to a culture of imagination and energy. If it does not, the business will die, or again be bought by another.

The ideas person is a different and much rarer beast than the founder of the business. The ideas person demonstrates all the talents of an entrepreneur, but is one who also realizes the worth of financial and management controls. The ideas person has considered the personal need for success. Is success needed because of a belief that success will bring security or is success desired because of a belief that success will bring independence? The ideas person knows that success may demand the forfeit of the very independence sought. By studying the desire for success, the ideas person identifies the parameters of the risks and the degree of independence that he or she is prepared to undertake in the hunt for success.

The ideas person also asks what is regarded as success. One's priorities are position, wealth, family unity and health, but not necessarily in that order. No risks will be taken that put any of these priorities in jeopardy, for the ideas person has thought about these issues and knows their value. The talents of the ideas person are acquired by long experience of business—experience of both triumph and failure.

The ideas person is one with a true love of business. Such a person has learned discipline and practices it as he or she captures companies. Such a person has a small staff who have served loyally for a long time, for the disruption of staff changes is costly. Such a person inspires loyalty because loyalty is given, and when times are hard, employer and staff stand shoulder to shoulder and loyalty works both ways. Only the pursuit of business rather than money can create and sustain real wealth. The quantity of money is merely the barometer used to measure success, pleasure is the reason that such a person goes on to become truly wealthy.

Do not buy a company from an ideas person, for you cannot improve the way it is run. Wait until that person's successors have had the company a year or more, then buy it and you will, with diligence, show a handsome return. Do not try to compete with such a person—rather become a friend and disciple. Study and learn, for knowledge of the human condition is everything in business.

Machiavelli's third course of action after acquiring a business is "to permit them to live under their own laws, drawing a tribute [dividend] and establishing within it an oligarchy which keeps it friendly to you." Machiavelli goes on to explain why this is a good course of action: "Because such a government being created by the Prince knows that it cannot stand without his friendship and interest, and does its utmost to support him; and therefore he who would keep a city [company] accustomed to freedom will hold it more easily by the means of its own citizens than in any other way."

Acquire a company that only you can see has an exciting future. Do not interfere with that company, but sell it when you see a profit or the danger of a loss. If you take this course of action, under no circumstances become friendly or even meet those who run that company, for their personal conditions must not be allowed to interfere with your decision to hold or to sell their company.

As discussed earlier, by far the most satisfactory course for the predator who would acquire a business is to find one that belongs to a family. The employees of the business are generally more susceptible to command once the family, who formerly controlled their affairs, are removed without trace. Machiavelli's advice is much the same. "When Cities [companies] or countries are accustomed to live under a prince, and his family is exterminated, they being on the one hand accustomed to obey and on the other hand, not having the old Prince, cannot agree in making one from amongst themselves and they do not know how to govern themselves. For this reason they are very slow to take up arms and a Prince can gain them to himself and secure them much more easily."

Directors of public companies, however, have had a taste of real power and will miss that power terribly. As Machiavelli wrote: "In republics [public companies] there is more vitality, greater hatred, and more desire for vengeance, which will never permit them to allow the memory of their former liberty to rest."

Machiavelli's solution is the same: "The safest way is to destroy them." The proprietor who acquires a business may well be tempted to keep in position a director of the former board who seems talented and obliging. Let that proprietor not be deceived, for, in time, that the talented and obliging director will be not only unobliging, but also show a talent for causing trouble. Whether the new proprietors be the entrepreneurs, the corporate managers or a person of ideas, the new proprietor must harden his or her heart and ensure that the actions taken in this newly acquired business must only be those that will further the success of the business. Whether the new proprietor does privately help those who face unjust adversity or adversity with which they cannot deal because they have been dismissed from the business, must be between the new proprietor and that proprietor's soul.

9

On Those who Acquire Principalities through Wicked Deeds.

STEALING A BUSINESS

Above all, a Prince should live with his subjects in such a way that no unforeseen circumstance, be it good or bad, compels him to alter his conduct. When, in times of adversity, necessity dictates, evil deeds are already too late, and good deeds of no use as they are judged forced, and not worthy of thanks.

In this passage, Machiavelli highlights the need to be constantly alert to the possibility of treachery, and warns that you should already have a reputation for taking terrible revenge before this treachery occurs. Because of this reputation, you can then afford to deal kindly with your employees.

Machiavelli is of the opinion that there are two ways that a person may rise to power, "neither of which can be entirely attributed to fortune or genius." Machiavelli describes these methods thus: "When either by some wicked or nefarious ways, one ascends to the principality or when, by favor of his fellow citizens, a private person becomes the prince of his country." Machiavelli quotes two examples; the first, a common soldier who rose to be King of Syracuse by becoming extremely good at his profession. However, this man was, by nature, treacherous. Never for one moment imagine that all treachery fails, or that all those who practice dishonesty are caught and punished. Having achieved a position of power, this man called together the senate and the important citizens of Syracuse, "As if he had to discuss with them things relating to the Republic, and at a given signal the soldiers killed all the Senators and the richest of the people." So Agathocles, the Sicilian son of a potter, became King of Syracuse.

To draw a parallel in a modern business, I use the apologue of the apparently obliging employee who willingly takes care of matters for his employer. Slowly this person consolidates his position, and the amiable employer, believing this man to be both honest and conscientious, leaves many matters to him. The obliging employee may very well carry out the task to the satisfaction of his employer, or if he does not, he will bury the matter so that his employer neither spots his failure, nor worries about the task that his man failed to perform. Slowly, as he carries out these tasks for his employer, he shapes his employer's business to his own image. For one day he plans to become the employer and that the amiable employer should become his employee. Little by little, the obliging employee gains an element of control within his employer's business. Usually this power base is financial. He will often form a relationship with the company's bankers, soon telling his employer that he cannot do this or that as the banks will not allow these actions to be taken, or that the banks insist on them taking this or that action. Many of these actions are carried out against both the instincts and the best interests of the amiable employer.

Such a man as the obliging employee is devious by nature and treacherous by inclination, and his chief talent is that of patience. Such a man as I have described will bring a company to ruin, for the obliging employee's agenda is different from that of his employer's. In order for him to succeed, the company must be short of funds, and companies that are over-extended are easy prey to villains who, when they gain control, will surely extend the finances of these companies further, so lining their own pockets.

In truth, it is the fault of the amiable employer if such people prosper, for good nature has no part to play in business. The amiable employer must seek out such people and dismiss them if only to encourage the honest people that are employed to continue on the path of honesty. He must take control of the company's finances, bowing to none in judgment of how they are run. The relationship between a company and its bank is the prerogative of the employer. He alone must have control of that relationship, otherwise he will become desperately vulnerable. Weakness only opens the way to your own destruction.

When times are hard, the ineffectual come into their own and rise to positions of power that are unimaginable in good times. These obliging servants explain away their incompetence by a lack of resources, and if by chance they should have any success, they claim more than their just credit. Any criticisms directed to them are nearly always neatly deflected on to others close to them. Their actions are only influenced by their desire for power, even if that power is over a small company, and it is their desire for safety that will destroy a company's prospects for the future.

Writing of Agathocles, Machiavelli states, "He who considers the actions and the genius of this man will see nothing or little which can be attributed to fortune." Machiavelli continues, "Yet it cannot be called talent to slay fellow citizens, to deceive friends, to be without faith; without mercy; without religion; such methods gain an empire, but not glory."

Success in business is worthless if it leaves the one who has succeeded without honor. Machiavelli wrote, again about Agathocles, "Consider that his ability to overcome obstacles and to endure hardship along with his courage in entering into dangers and extracting himself from them" qualify him, so that "it cannot be seen why he should be esteemed less than the most notable Captain." Thus, Machiavelli shows his admiration for success, and his view that to succeed is the arbiter of success predates an American business attitude by nearly four hundred years. For fame and success are the touchstones by which one is judged in America today, where both fame and success lead to wealth and wealth so often leads to greater fame and greater success.

Before considering Machiavelli's next example, it is worth dwelling for a moment on Agathocles's treatment of the senators of Syracuse. Right through *The Prince* Machiavelli gives examples of how to gain the upper hand; however, almost inevitably, they nearly always require the extermination of competitors and displaced princes. Although this may have been common in the fifteenth century, it is not a practical way to proceed while conducting business in the closing years of the twentieth century. Now the enemy is left around to take revenge at a later date. As explained, wherever possible, promote your enemies, and through this promotion make their positions untenable. Turn your enemies into the objects of jealousy. As they criticize you, they will be seen as ungrateful and therefore have less public credibility.

Nevertheless, the problem of an ever-increasing circle of enemies remains for the one who would rise in the ranks of any business. Remember that when a person leaves a company, they are not totally without influence in that company. In all walks of life, friendships will be made that transcend circumstances, friendships that endure long after a person has changed their employment. Beware the dismissed employee who still has friends among your existing employees and beware the relatives of the dismissed employee, for you may find them among your customers, or the employees of your customers.

For Machiavelli's second example, he takes the case of Oliverotto da Ferro, who, left an orphan, was brought up by Giovanni Foglianni. Trained as a soldier, he became "the first man in his profession." This man determined no longer to serve under others, in much the same way that the obliging employee determines to take his employer's business and so serve only himself. Da Ferro wrote to Giovanni Foglianni, the man who had cared for him in his youth and suggested that, as he had been away from home for many years, he should visit Foglianni and his city. Da Ferro would, he said, as a matter of honor, bring with him one hundred horsemen, in order to show Foglianni's fellow citizens that the man whom Foglianni loved had become a personage of consequence. After considerable feasting and friendship, da Ferro's men murdered their hosts. Taking control of the city, da Ferro "killed all the Malcontents who were able to injure him and strengthened himself with new civil and military ordinances." So secure did da Ferro become in his city that he became a threat to his neighbors and one year later he was strangled. A cheat so often imagines that the rules when changed by cheating have only been changed for the benefit of that cheat. Little do they realize that once the rules have been changed by cheating, others will be encouraged to play by these new rules.

Machiavelli speculates on the success of Agathocles and the failure of da Ferro. He concludes that Agathocles succeeded because he made the state he stole successful, yet da Ferro failed because he did not allow for the jealousy of his neighbors. The treachery gave both these men only the opportunity to succeed, but treachery in its own right does not guarantee success. Machiavelli writes: "I believe that this follows from severities being badly or properly used. Those may be called properly used, if of evil it is lawful to speak well, that are applied at one blow and are necessary to one's security, and that are not persisted in afterwards unless they can be turned to the advantage of the subjects. The badly employed are, those which notwithstanding they may be few in the commencement, multiply with time rather than decrease." Machiavelli, in this passage, admits to degrees in dishonesty, whereas in reality, dishonesty should be seen in the same light as pregnancy—you cannot be a little bit pregnant, nor a little bit dishonest. The terms are both definite and that is how they must be treated.

Good intentions in business, as in life, are so often the root of the evil that grows from them. In business there must be no ambiguity. Theft, both large and small, must be stamped out. Dishonesty on a small scale in a company can be extremely expensive, not for the sums that are stolen, rather for the cost of covering up the fact that those sums have been stolen. Theft on a large scale is expensive because a company that has been stolen from its rightful owners will never have honor, however successful that company is, and as for the cost of that theft, it is paid for by those who were not party to that theft by losing their jobs.

Conducting business is a stern affair, and Machiavelli sums it all up when he describes how to deal with the citizens of a conquered state or the subjects of a prince who has just come to power. "Injuries ought to be done all at one time, so that, being tasted less, they offend less. Benefits ought to be given little by little, so that the flavour of them may last longer."

10

On Civil Principalities.

RISING TO POWER

When a private citizen becomes Prince of his land with the support of his fellow citizens rather than through wickedness or intolerable violence.

The employee who would rise to control a business by stealth is not to be confused with the obliging employee who would steal a business by treachery, despite the fact that they have many characteristics in common—patience and determination to name but a few. The obliging employee is only self-interested and as such will lack both courage and honor, two qualities without which it is impossible to use fairly the power that goes with the control of a business. Nor will the obliging employee use that power to the advantage of both the employer and employees, let alone those with whom business is done, clients and customers, and least of all, those unconnected to the business, but whose lives are affected by the action of the business. If this last category of people is neglected, they can cause endless damage, for they can devote a large amount of time to destroying a small part of your business, and the destruction of that small part can damage the whole.

To rise to power in a business it is necessary to have access to the world of business. Education is but one way to gain such access. It should be remembered that many of the greatest business successes have received little formal education.

When applying for a job, do it on the employer's terms. Seek the job that is offered rather than the job to which you feel you are entitled and acquire a reputation for efficiency while doing that job. Study the business that you have joined; the lower the capacity that you serve in, the more time you will have for that study. Most important of all, demonstrate determination and commitment: qualities that will allow you to rise in your chosen occupation. The world of business seems to be a hard place in which to succeed, but, in the fact, the reverse is true. If a new employee demonstrates complete commitment to that aim that employee will succeed. Many employees may dream of one day running the business where they work but seldom are they prepared to spend the time and energy required to achieve this. The sacrifice of life's many pleasures is for them far too great, the fear of responsibilities far too onerous. These employees, who are by far the majority, find that they are happy just to be employed.

Machiavelli suggests that an employee can rise to power "by the favour of his fellow citizens," and continues, "nor is genius or fortune altogether necessary to attain to it, but rather a happy shrewdness." He states that such a principality [business] is obtained either by the favor of the people [shareholders] or by the favor of the nobles [executive board members] Machiavelli points out that there is always a tension between these two parties and where there is a tension, however well disguised, there is always the possibility of a rift. The shareholders wish to make money, but in general do not wish to control the business. The executive directors wish the business to make profits, but primarily the directors wish to profit from their labors. They seek rewards quite apart from their salaries, often in the form of stock options or the like. The shareholders have purchased their stake in the business while the executive directors wish to earn their stake. "From these two opposite desires, there arises in cities [businesses] one of these results—either a Principality [a business run on patriarchal lines and run by the shareholders, some of whom are employed in that business]; self government [a business run with the maximum of consultation upwards and downwards] or anarchy." Machiavelli goes on, "a principality [business] is created by either the people or the nobles, according as one or other of them has the opportunity." In this case, the shareholders are those who own and run the business. The relative positions and powers of shareholders and executive directors must be well understood by the employee who would rise in the ranks of those employed by the business.

Machiavelli accepts the diversity of these two parties— shareholders and non-executive directors—and the incipient drama of that situation. He then sets about clearing a pathway through this jungle to the ambition of the employee who would rule. "The nobles seeing they cannot withstand the people [shareholders] begin to cry up the reputation of one of themselves and they make him a Prince [chairperson], so that under his shadow they can give vent to their ambitions." Machiavelli continues, "The people [shareholders] finding they cannot trust the nobles, also cry up the reputation of one of themselves and make him a Prince [chairperson], so as to be defended by his Authority." Here Machiavelli has advice for the employee who rises by stealth: "He who obtains sovereignty by the assistance of the nobles, maintains himself with more difficulty than he who comes to it by the aid of the people, because the former finds himself with many around him who consider themselves his equals, and because of this he can neither rule nor manage them to his liking." The employee who rises in this fashion is in office, but not in power. This chairperson can only draw wages and direct at the whim of the executive directors. Machiavelli continues: "But he who reached sovereignty by popular favour, finds himself alone and has none around him, or few, who are not prepared to obey him. Besides this, one cannot by fair dealing and without injury to others satisfy the Nobles. But you can satisfy the people for their object is more righteous than the Nobles'." However, whether the object of the people is more righteous than that of the nobles must be in question. The object for the shareholder is much more straightforward. Their object is pure profit.

Thus Machiavelli outlines the way to the top, but as often in Machiavelli's work, these matters are not that easily understood, for he continues, "It is to be added also that a Prince can never secure himself against a hostile people, because of them being too many, whilst from the Nobles he can secure himself as they are few in number." In other words, in the end the shareholders will have their way.

The next piece of Machiavelli's advice is to describe a situation that so often besets the employee who would rise, and it is the reason why such an employee needs courage. In a matter-of-fact way, Machiavelli states, "The worst that a Prince may expect from a hostile people is to be abandoned by them." In time, the shareholders will sack the employee who has risen. Nobles, however, are a different kettle of fish. "From hostile Nobles he has not only to fear abandonment, but also that they will rise against him [destroy his reputation], for they being in these affairs more by far seeing and astute, always look forward in time to save themselves and to obtain favours from him whom they expect to prevail. Further, the Prince is compelled to live [to work] always with the same people, but he can do well without the same nobles, being able to make and unmake them daily and to give or take away authority when it pleases him."

Here Machiavelli points out that the chairperson can change the board, but it is harder to change the shareholders, and that in any case such changes seldom are to the long-term advantage of the chairperson. So should the aspiring employee ignore the nobles and concentrate on the people? This seems to be what Machiavelli advises—but does he? He writes, "Therefore one who becomes a Prince through the favour of the people ought to keep them friendly and this he can easily do seeing they only ask not to be oppressed [robbed of profits] by him. But one who in opposition to the people becomes a Prince by favour of the nobles, ought above everything to seek to win the people over to himself and this he may easily do if he takes them under his protection. Because when they receive good from him of whom they were expecting evil, they are bound more closely to their Benefactor, thus the people quickly become more devoted to him than if he had been raised to the principality by their favours." In fact, Machiavelli is advising the aspiring employee to ally himself with the nobles on the way to power. However, the moment that aspiring employees become the employers, they must, without delay, change their position and their loyalty. The people [shareholders] have become the employers' natural ally, and without them the employers cannot run their businesses.

In business, as in politics, the matter of loyalty is an abstract quality. Most probably it is best demonstrated by a faithful dog. In humans, loyalty has far greater implications. Loyalty to an idea or cause can embrace loyalty to the individual who leads that cause. When, however, that leader moves away from that cause, loyalty should remain with the cause. Loyalty is not a fact to be relied upon. Employees who have worked loyally, while events were to their advantage, will believe themselves loyal. When events change, the same people will rationalize loyalty and introduce the notion of comparative loyalty. First loyalties, those people will argue, are to spouses and families, when in reality they serve only themselves. In truth, they have never been loyal in the first place: their apparent loyalty is a fiction in the imagination of both employer and employee. The aspiring employee must remember that loyalty is a constituent of honor, an inconvenience that must be suffered if an honorable goal is to be achieved. Equally, aspiring employees will realize that honor may not be the touchstone of those around them, and that many people use loyalty merely as a prop to their own self-esteem.

The amiable employer will govern through others and, when he chooses others, apparent loyalty is likely to be a quality that he puts ahead of ability. The obliging employee, who seeks a speedy way to power, seldom realizes the value that employer puts on loyalty. Being a man of no principle, the obliging employee seeing the employer removed from power, will desert his employer and seek employment elsewhere. Little does this formerly obliging employee realize that the finest advertisement he could have for a new position is to demonstrate the greatest loyalty of staying at the side of the employer removed from power, for in doing this the employee will demonstrate the quality that great Princes seek and seldom find. Machiavelli writes, "For such a Prince cannot rely upon what he observes in quiet time, when citizens have need of the state, because then every one agrees with him; they all promise and when death is far distant, they all wish to die for him; but in troubled times, when the state has need of its citizens, then he finds but few."

To succeed, the aspiring employee must prove to be one of the few who does not fail when faced with trouble, one of the few who, when the employer is in dire straits, does not desert and does not plunder the employer's business. Machiavelli writes, "Nobis, Prince of Sparta sustained the attack of all Greece and of a victorious Roman army, and against these he defended his country and his government; and for the overcoming of this Peril it was only necessary for him to make himself secure against a few, but this would not have been sufficient if the people had been hostile, and do not let any impugn the statement with the trite Proverb, He who builds on the people [employees], builds on Mud. For this is true when a private citizen makes a foundation there and persuades himself that the people will free him when he is oppressed by his enemies or the Magistrates." He continues, "A Prince who has established himself as above 'Nobis, Prince of Sparta,' who can command and is a man of courage undismayed in adversity, who does not fail in other qualifications and who by his resolution and energy keeps the whole people encouraged. Such a one will never find himself deceived in the end and will be shown that he has laid his foundations well." This can be taken to mean that those who would run a company should demonstrate these qualities to their supporters, banks, shareholders and junior management. To have the confidence of banks is vitally important during hard times.

Furthermore, they who would run a company should put little trust in their executive directors. Machiavelli writes, "These principalities [companies] are liable to danger when they are passing from the civil to the absolute order of Government, for such Princes either rule personally, or through Magistrates." The amiable employer chooses to rule through the obliging employee [magistrates]. "In the latter case the Government is weaker and more insecure, because it rests entirely on the goodwill of those citizens who are raised to the Magistracy and who, especially in troubled times, can destroy the Government with great ease by intrigue or open defiance; and the Prince has not the chance amid tumults to exercise absolute authority because the citizens and the subjects [employees] are accustomed to receive orders from the Magistrates and are not of a mind to obey him amid all these confusions, and there will always be in doubtful times a scarcity of men whom he can trust."

Let not the aspiring employees fall into the trap of believing themselves to be the chairperson and so behave like a chairperson when they are, in reality, only employees who have not yet earned that high position. Also let not the aspiring employees fall into the trap of believing that the success that the business enjoys is entirely due to their own efforts and that the employer does nothing, for the employee who takes such a view does not fully understand the business. Such an employee is better dismissed sooner than later, both for the employee's own benefit and the benefit of the employer.

The aspiring employees must realize that they are not yet in power and conduct themselves with modesty, for many a plan cunningly conceived has been brought to nothing by the jealousy of colleagues. Let the aspiring employees realize that power in a business really lies with the telephonists, the chairman's secretary and the cleaners. Their words reach the ears of those who can promote. Small actions by these people can kill the chances of those who seek promotion. Human nature being what it is, these people can spot with certainty the difference between ambition and dedication and, having time to spare, their instinct is to thwart ambition and to respect dedication. Never speak evil of one colleague to another for that other colleague will without doubt pass on the words that you have spoken, particularly if they are sworn to secrecy.

The employees who will rise in the ranks of other employees, and in the end command, must have the qualities of leadership, courage, initiative and, above all, the ability of invention. Such aspiring employees must conduct themselves with honor, while the greatest tool at the disposal of aspiring employees is politeness. I point out no easy path towards the control of people and companies. The apprenticeship to power is hard but far harder when that power must be achieved with honor. However, the final achievement of position and power with honor is without price. For honor can never be attached to position and power at a later date.

11

On the Different Types of Army and the Question of Mercenary Troops.

THE USE OF CONSULTANTS

Now that I have discussed in detail the characteristics of those principalities that I set out to consider at the start, and having considered to some extent the reasons for their well-being and their ill health and shown the means employed by many to acquire and keep hold of them, it now remains for me to discuss in a general manner the offensive and defensive strategies that can occur in each of the forms mentioned above

Having taken from Machiavelli some advice that pertains to the process of taking over another business, now it is time to consider how his advice may be used and what steps must be taken to defend your business from hostile takeover.

"We have seen above how necessary it is for a Prince to have his foundations well laid, otherwise it follows, of necessity, he will go to ruin." In business, the "foundations" to which Machiavelli refers apply not only to having the funds available to sustain either attack or defense, but also to having employees who are reliable both in defense and attack. Takeovers are not just about assets, they are also about people; the people that you employ and the people employed by the company that you would take over. Furthermore, takeovers are about all the other people whose lives are affected by the change of ownership of a business and the inevitable change in the style of how that business is managed.

Looking first at the people that you employ, it would be wise to consider an example of a grave mistake made by the amiable employer. In the days when his business flourished, he employed an able lieutenant. Slowly as the years passed, his trust in this able lieutenant grew and he handed more and more responsibility to him. Such responsibility was of a limited nature—perhaps the best word to describe that responsibility would be "authority," for although the able lieutenant had the authority to decide some matters, his responsibility was limited to the carrying out of the employer's orders. He was not concerned with the wisdom of the decision in the first place. The amiable employer took the responsibility for the welfare of the whole undertaking. It is important to understand the two natures of responsibility: first, the responsibility to carry out a function and second, the responsibility for a function once it has been carried out. The second is far more onerous, and so allows the employee who carries out the first both freedom and peace of mind.

For many years the relationship between the amiable employer and his able lieutenant prospered, until, as always happens, events took a downturn. Business became hard and tiresome, the able lieutenant became uncertain of his future and left the employ of his amiable employer to find secure employment with a government department. When considering who was to take over the role of the able lieutenant, the obvious choice seemed to be the obliging employee, who was always lurking near at hand. In truth, the amiable employer had always had doubts about the ability of the obliging employee. These doubts he put on one side at the behest of the able lieutenant, whose interest was to ease his departure and his conscience at leaving his amiable employer when times were troubled. Having found his replacement, the able lieutenant left without delay. This solution might indeed have worked if the amiable employer had not made one mistake, and this is the mistake I warn you of when replacing staff. Instead of making the obliging employee start at the levels of trust, responsibility and authority where the able lieutenant had started, the amiable employer allowed this devious and cunning, but apparently obliging, employee to start at the levels of trust, responsibility and authority already reached by the able lieutenant. This mistake put a man filled with guile and treachery into a position of great power.

It may seem that the amiable employer had little choice in the matter. Should he instead have hired a person little known to him from outside his business? Machiavelli has strong views on the use of mercenaries and auxiliaries. "I say therefore that the arms with which a Prince defends his state are either his own or they are mercenaries, auxiliaries or mixed. Mercenaries and auxiliaries are useless and dangerous and if one holds his state based on these arms, he will stand neither firm nor safe; for they are disunited, ambitious and without discipline, unfaithful, valiant before friends, cowardly before enemies. They have neither the fear of God, nor fidelity to Men, and destruction is deferred only as long as attack is: for in peace one is robbed by them and in war by the enemy." Trust must be built up over the years and should not be assumed to be present at first acquaintance. Years of employment, however, do not equate to trust. Trust is a personal emotion and trust only truly works if it is found to flow in both directions.

Auxiliaries and mercenaries can be updated to twentieth-century terms by reference to new employees and consultants. The amiable employer might well have resolved his dilemma by employing a mercenary, for such people exist in business. They move from one organization to another, finding employment when there are troubled times, taking their bags of gold and moving on. More usually than not they leave the business apparently restored to safety, but in fact either altered beyond belief or still in jeopardy. "The principle that has guided them has been first to lower the credit of infantry so that they might increase their own. They did this because subsisting on their pay and without territory, they were unable to support many soldiers, and a few infantry did not give them any authority. So they were led to employ cavalry, with a moderate force of which they were maintained and honoured." These people change the rules, and given their way, they dismiss old employees and bring in new. In general, they run matters to suit their own convenience. "They had, besides this, used every art to lessen fatigue and danger to themselves, and their soldiers, not killing in the fray, but taking prisoners and liberating without ransom. They did not attack towns at night, nor did the garrisons of the towns attack encampments at night; they did not surround the camp either with stockade or ditch, nor did they campaign in the winter."

Mercenaries take short-term measures to make short-term profit. Both for themselves and the businesses that they are supposed to save, they make matters seem as if they are under control when in fact they are not. They do not take the actions that are needed to produce long-term profit, so the businesses that they claim to have saved will not prosper in years to come. The future of those businesses has been exchanged for the convenience of the present.

Beware the brilliant young man or woman brought in to help you out of your trouble, for there are many examples of amiable employers being helped out of their jobs. Whether or not these brilliant mercenaries are treacherous at the beginning, as they begin to understand the size of the prize, and the ease with which they can win, and as contempt for their employer grows in their hearts, so their treachery grows. When they feel that an employer has put a business in jeopardy from which they alone have saved it, their treachery is based on the belief that they are right in their actions and what they intend to do is just. This is the most dangerous type of treachery of all.

"I wish to demonstrate further the infelicity of these arms. The mercenary captains are either capable men, or they are not; if they are, you cannot trust them, because they always aspire to their own greatness, either by oppressing you, who are their master, or others contrary to your intentions; but if the Captain is not skilful, you are ruined in the usual way." Machiavelli uses two historical examples to demonstrate his point: "Philip of Macedon was made Captain of the Soldiering by the Thebans and after victory he took away their liberty," and also "Duke Filippo being dead, the Milanese enlisted Francesco Sforza against the Venetians and he having overcome the enemy at Caravaggio allied himself with them to crush the Milanese."

Machiavelli's stories are a warning against employing consultants to set a business back on its course. Consultants have one use and that is the producing of evidence about how a business is run. It does not, in fact, matter whether their evidence is accurate or not—the very effort needed to produce the evidence is enough to start those who work in a business thinking about how that business is run. The accuracy of the evidence is in the hands of those who formulate that evidence and they will either see the defects in how they manage the business and take action, or ignore them, justifying the defects to themselves. In any event, to irritate is to stimulate and the consultants will have done both of these things. So often truth comes out of mistaken evidence, or as Machiavelli wrote: "He who told us that our sins were the cause of it told the Truth, but they were not the sins that he imagined." In fact, businesses must be run by those charged with running them, who in turn must take the responsibility of running that business. They should not bring in outsiders whom they do not know, or promote those of little ability but great treachery. The amiable employer should have foreseen the day that the able lieutenant might go and have prepared a plan to deal with such a situation.

In bringing in outsiders to help a business in peril, again one who runs that business must anticipate treachery. The employer should ensure he is making use of the brilliant mercenary, rather than allow the mercenary to use the business for the mercenary's own advancement. Actions must be taken if such a person is employed to limits beyond that person's powers. That person must not be allowed anywhere near the banks who finance the business, nor the shareholders who own the business. The mercenary may reorganize, but only to an agreed plan, and it must be made clear to the other employees that no real power lies in the mercenary's hands. A brilliant mercenary, contemplating treachery, will not accept such terms; an honest mercenary, with a clear conscience, will accept them because such a mercenary will expect that this task will have parameters.

The fundamental truth is, however, that if you cannot run your own business, give it up. As Machiavelli states, "As they were the sins of Princes, it is the Princes who must also suffer the penalty."

Let us now consider the people who are employed by those who have been successful in taking over businesses where they work. Some who are experts in taking over businesses make a point of never meeting those whom they now employ. They do this firstly because they may have to sack their new employees, and to know them might cause personal embarrassment, and also because they do not want to be influenced by the new employees' views, for a takeover without a change of style in the way that the taken-over company is run does not exist. Others take a different stance and get to know well those that they now control. However, beware of this strategy, for new employees often seem better able to carry out their work than old employees. Never allow newcomers to persuade you of anything against your better judgment. New employees are, as far as you are concerned, merely auxiliaries, and they have all the qualities and dangers of auxiliaries. Machiavelli writes, "The Venetians if their achievements are considered, will be seen to have acted safely and gloriously, so long as they sent to war their own men, when with armed gentlemen and plebeians they did valiantly. This was before they turned to enterprises on land, but when they began to fight on land, they forsook this virtue and followed the custom of Italy." They hired mercenaries and auxiliaries.

In a business this would happen when expansion went on apace and the parent company had neither the resources, human or financial, to deal with the situation that was developing. In such circumstances, each new takeover is intended to set a dangerous situation right, but in fact, makes it even more dangerous. Machiavelli continues, with a parallel of the expansion of the Venetian Empire, to chart the course of many expanding companies: "And in the beginning of the expansion on land, though not having much territory, and because of their great reputation, they had not much to fear from the captains; but when they expanded, as under Carmignuola they had a taste of this mistake; for having found him a most valiant man [they beat the Duke of Milan under his leadership] and on the other hand knowing

85

how lukewarm he was in the war, they feared they would no longer conquer under him, and for this reason they were not willing, nor were they able, to let him go; and so not to lose again that which they had acquired." The Venetians had hired a brilliant commander who had made them rich by acquisition. They had no loyalty to him and so suspected that he had no loyalty to them. They were certain that if he left their employ then he would take back the empire that he had won for them, and give that empire to other employers. The Venetians' solution was to murder the man.

In business, the best way to deal with this matter is to avoid it in the first place, by knowing that a situation can develop. If, in ignorance, you allow such a person to occupy a position of power and you need to get rid of that person, the only modern way to do this is to lobby politicians to find that employee a job that will bring about the employee's removal with honor. No doubt, you will have already made this employee rich and money alone will not satisfy such a person — this person's mind needs to be engaged and his or her conceit satisfied. An important position, the likes of which are in the gift of governments, is the ideal solution to your problem. Never fall into the trap of sending an intelligent employee into the desert of secondment, for being intelligent, that employee will prosper there and still be a threat to you.

Always improve the situation of those you wish to get rid of, for murder is not a twentieth-century option. If destruction is needed — and bear in mind that destruction is only needed in a last resort or when dealing with treachery — destroy absolutely. Do not under any circumstances turn back once a course of destruction has been embarked upon. Neither mercy nor charity should be shown to those who would act treacherously, for mercy and charity shown to such people are interpreted as symptoms of weakness, and weakness is the quality upon which the treacherous thrive. Weakness opens the door to your own destruction.

Last, let us take the case of those who are affected by the takeover of a business in the broadest sense—those who find that the business's products increase in price and are enraged at the dealings of the stockmarkets of the world that seem to rob them of their wages. In the end, unfettered capitalism is like an uncontrolled truck, it will crash and bring down with it those who profit most from that capitalism. The fetters of capitalism should be a sense of responsibility exercised by those engaged in commerce, not laws invented by governments.

It is the restrictions placed on businesses by governments that allow those well versed in the meaning and implications of these restrictions to profit, but these restrictions slow the whole process of trade. While there must be controls to safeguard those who invest and those who shop for goods and services, wise governments keep such restrictions and controls to the very minimum. Controls, however, are not enough and the intentions of those who would take over others must be good. If those who run great industries do not act responsibly, eventually they put the whole principle of capitalism in jeopardy.

The one who takes over another must consider what effect the new ownership and style of management will have on the environment in which that business operates and also the effect the new ownership will have on employment in the district where that business is located. Such benefits must be published, for, in attack, allies must be recruited and, as we know well, takeovers are not just about money. One who takes over should also be aware that there are responsibilities to other organizations in the district and also to charities. Both those who work for a business and those who live near a business center must be made to believe that the new owners intend to put a part of what they take out back into that business and into the community. With these allies on the ground, the views of distant shareholders who need only consider money can be influenced. That which seems an expansive plan can turn out, properly marshaled, to be money well spent.

Machiavelli, where he writes of war, exactly catches the nature of business, particularly when he writes of the fate of the Venetian Empire. "In one battle they lost that which in eight hundred years they had acquired with so much trouble. Because from such arms conquests come but slowly, long delayed and inconsiderable, but losses sudden and portentous."

12

On Auxiliary Troops, your own Troops, and a Mixture of the Two.

THE NEED FOR LOYALTY

Auxiliary troops, which are the second kind of useless soldier, are those sent when you ask a powerful ruler to help to defend you with his troops. Pope Julius did this recently when, having observed his mercenary force's poor performance during the Ferrara campaign, he turned to auxiliaries and arranged for the soldiers and armies of Ferdinand, King of Spain, to help him. These troops can be useful and effective in their own right. However, they are almost always harmful to those who have recourse to them, as if they lose, you are undone; if they win, you become their prisoner.

Machiavelli continuously warns against both mercenaries and auxiliaries, for they have no loyalty and loyalty is of the utmost priority when you are assessing those that you employ. Such loyalty is an emotion far deeper than that of facile loyalty. Employees, when they wish to gain your confidence, will speak of loyalty in general terms. The loyalty which an employer should be concerned with springs from shared beliefs and a community of interest. This form of loyalty has as its constituents, courage and determination; it is not the loyalty of habit. This loyalty is not a cheap commodity, easily picked up and just as easily put down again. A deep loyalty is a commitment to another person or idea, despite the flaws in that idea or the other person's character. It is the support of a person when they are wrong, when they are truculent and most of all when they are destroyed and unable to benefit you. In reality, such loyalty only becomes necessary when belief in the person or their idea is dead.

This deep loyalty some might call love, for love has all the constituents of deep loyalty with one exception. Love as the name for such a quality has a strange connotation when used in the context of business. People are afraid to use such a word and regard it as too precious to be used in the context of commerce. Loyalty is of particular importance in those you employ who are closest to you. I have already written about the able lieutenant and his great loyalty when times were good and his desertion in pursuit of self-interest when times were hard, leaving the amiable employer's business exposed to the wiles of the obliging employee. Neither man had a concept of deep loyalty. Both wore loyalty as a badge, taking pleasure in the prestige that their loyalty brought them, caring nothing for that loyalty in reality, or the liabilities that such loyalty carried. Deep loyalty must be given and it must be understood to have been given by both parties, for it flows in both directions. In times of sickness and health, in matters private and public, in good times and bad, the employer must be concerned for the employee, and the employee must be concerned about the employer.

It is of the utmost importance to recognize those who are disloyal and even more important to recognize those who have disloyalty as a part of their character. Then it is merely judgment that will tell you at which point their flamboyant loyalty will lurch into treachery. They are among the most destructive people that you will encounter, and could, if your judgment of their character is flawed, bring about your downfall.

The amiable employer made his first mistake when he chose an able lieutenant and trusted him more than he should, without considering whether this man was weak or strong. The second mistake came when the amiable employer promoted the obliging employee. The amiable employer did not consider the characters of these two employees and how those characters would change as circumstances change. This is perhaps the most important aspect of the individuals that you might employ. Neither the amiable employer nor the able lieutenant knew how the other would act under the stress of impending disaster, for neither had seen the other in such a situation. In the case of the obliging employee, it is possible that closer examination of his character would have revealed the greed and ambition that made him so treacherous. These instincts are present in all our souls, some of us are naturally strong, some of us naturally weak and some of us naturally treacherous. Only pressure and stress will reveal the baser instincts of mankind, separating them from the camouflages of friendship, good fellowship, courtesy and apparent consideration.

The amiable employer, being lazy by nature and careless over detail, neglected to reflect on the characters of these two men. It is in small actions that people betray themselves and these small actions are the hints, the symptoms of the hidden parts of their character. You will only discover these small hints after years of familiarity. Therefore, despite the fact that there are apparently more important matters for the employer to deal with, employers must under no circumstances relax their vigilance on their close employees. They should always be looking for a hint to reveal the truth. From such a close interest will grow the deep loyalty, perhaps called love, and with that loyalty, total trust.

Trust, the companion of loyalty, is based on integrity in all actions. Do not expect those you employ to put their trust in you, if you do not trust them. Do not expect them to steal for you and not to steal from you. Do not expect them to break their pledges to others, because it is convenient for you, and not to break their pledges to you. As trust grows between employer and employee, so grows the great loyalty. Furthermore, the employer must trust the employee to do the best that the employee can, and if that employee fails because of promotion above that employee's ability, then the employer must be prepared to admit to the blame. Above all, never blame an employee for your own mistakes. Rather, take the blame for your employee's mistakes and then take the matter up with that employee in private — never humiliate an employee by a public rebuke. An employer needs to be scrupulously fair. All criticism of employees must be private to those employees, and that criticism must be objective, based on fact, not on hearsay and rumor. There must be respect at all times. The employee must respect the employer and the employer in turn must respect the employee, for if you do not respect another they will not respect you.

An employee who refuses to carry out the policy of the company because that employee considers the company's systems ridiculous or unnecessary, or an employee who refuses to cooperate with others is totally unacceptable and must be dismissed sooner rather than later. In this employee's dismissal may well lie trouble but not as much trouble as if such an employee is kept. It is far better to deal with such matters right at the beginning rather than putting them off, hoping that in time they will go away. As I have written before, and as Machiavelli repeats endlessly in his work *The Prince*, do not be tempted to change old friends for new, no matter how clever the new ones appear to be, and never allow newcomers to persuade you against your better judgment, and in particular against those who have given you their deep loyalty.

Never shirk from your responsibility. If employees must be dismissed through no fault of their own, send them away with honor. If their dismissal will cause them and their family hardship, but is necessary for the good of the business and the remainder of those employed there, then that dismissal must be made and the employee concerned helped privately by the employer. The employer has a larger responsibility to employees than merely managing the business. If, on the other hand, the employee must be dismissed for reasons which are the employee's fault, the good of the company must be considered and that employee, however unjustified it may be, must be sent away feeling well-disposed towards the company and the company should pay the cost of this action. If, however, this employee has caused the company harm, then that employee must be dismissed and fought, regardless of the cost both in money and in reputation. If not, the employee will become a model for others to imitate.

Never fail to express your appreciation and gratitude to others and never pretend that their ideas are yours. Let your employees take full credit for their efforts. Never be afraid to make firm and unpopular decisions, for nothing so weakens both a business and those who run a business, than decisions which change with the wind. Such actions will only bring temporary popularity at the expense of long-term contempt. Nothing so destabilizes a business as decisions that are constantly changed, and nothing costs a company more than the time wasted in constantly changing decisions.

Finally, when employing people, above all be your own person. Remember the writings of Machiavelli: "I wish also to recall to memory an instance from the Old Testament applicable to this subject. David offered himself to Saul to fight with Goliath, the Philistine Champion, and to give him courage, Saul armed him with his own weapons; which David rejected as soon as he had them on his back, saying he could make no use of them and that he wished to meet the enemy with his sling and his knife. In conclusion, the arms of others either fall from your back or weigh you down, or bind you fast."

13

On Cruelty and Mercy; and Whether it is Better to be Loved than Feared, or the Reverse.

MANAGING PEOPLE

Passing down the list of aforementioned qualities, I maintain that each Prince should desire to be thought merciful and not cruel. Nonetheless, he should be careful not to misuse this mercy.

Clemency is a commodity that should be administered in small doses. If clemency plays a large part in your style of management, then you will fall into the same trap that caught the amiable employer. Finding his employee obliging he allowed that employee far greater rein than was good for either of them. The amiable employer treated the inefficiencies of the obliging employee with clemency, believing that he was acting in the company's best interests. Meanwhile, the obliging employee, becoming used to clemency, became careless in his ways and took this clemency for granted. In time, the obliging employee began to resent any intrusion into his running of business, seeing it as unwarranted interference. Furthermore, he resented the fact that the amiable employer could intrude into what by now he regarded as his own.

Avoid clemency, as attractive as it may be to wallow in the admiration and the apparent love of your employees, such admiration and love is based on false premises. "Because this is to be asserted in general of men, that they are ungrateful, fickle, false, cowardly, covetous and as long as you succeed, they are yours entirely; they will offer you then blood, property, life and children, as is said above when the need is far distant; but when it approaches they turn against you. The Prince who was relying entirely on their promises and has neglected other precautions is ruined."

It is better for employees to tell their employer when they disagree. When telling their employer, however, employees must always remember that in the end, regardless of their views, the employer has the right to decide. The employee, should there be a disagreement, only has the right to seek employment elsewhere.

Machiavelli argues that it is kind to be cruel in a certain degree and probably to the advantage of princes to have a reputation that indicates their capacity for cruelty should the necessity arise. "Therefore a Prince so long as he keeps his subjects united and loyal [holds together his employees and has them working for the same ends] ought not to mind the reproach of cruelty; because with a few examples [of cruelty] he will be more merciful than those who through too much mercy, allow disorders to arise from which follow murders or robberies; for these are wont to injure the whole people whilst those executions which originate with a Prince offend the individual only."

The correct posture for an employer is one of strict fairness: dealing fairly with all employees, a fairness uncolored by personal likes or dislikes, uncluttered by self-interest. Such a fairness should have a clear set of boundaries which are well known to all concerned, and anyone who steps outside the boundaries should accept the consequences. As well as a reputation for fairness and, where necessary, cruelty, an employer should also have a reputation for kindness. This kindness should color every word and deed of the employer, and should become the standard by which employees treat each other. This kindness seeks to overcome the natural instincts of humans.

Machiavelli states, "And of all Princes, it is impossible for the new Prince to avoid the reputation of cruelty, owing to new states being full of dangers." My interpretation of Machiavelli's words refers to a new managing director of a business—a person recently appointed and unknown to new colleagues. Such a person will more often than not be too harsh or too kind, having no reputation except one brought from another place. It would be far better if such a promotion is made from within an organization for two reasons. First, the promotion encourages those others who work there, and second, the hiatus of uncertainty while employees adjust to their new master is avoided. A person promoted from within will often fall into the trap of being overly cruel or overly kind, but the damage will be far more minimal than that at the hands of a stranger.

Newly appointed executives must tread with caution and never ignore those who already occupy positions that are now inferior to their own. Such executives should never allow themselves to be rushed, but should carefully choose the right time to implement any changes. By being scrupulously fair and allowing employees time to change, the executive insures that the employees will adapt to the new style of business. Once having judged them carefully, then is the time for cruelty. If, however, cruelty must be exercised on those whose personal positions are vulnerable, then this is also the time for kindness. Such kindness will encourage and reassure other employees. Kindness, however, must never step in the way of corporate success, for corporate success involves the futures of all employees. The kindness must be exercised in a way that does not affect the business engaged in.

Always remember that the one who has recently taken over control of a business will be accused of many things. Time is the commodity that such a one needs, for time is a great healer. Machiavelli writes, "Nevertheless he ought to be slow to believe and to act, nor should he himself show fear, but proceed in a temperate manner with prudence and humanity so that too much confidence may not make him incautious and too much distrust render him intolerable." Machiavelli here can be considered to examine the relationship between employee and employer. "Because friendships that one obtained by payments and not by greatness or nobility of mind, may indeed be earned, but they are not secured and in time cannot be relied upon; and men have less scruple in offending one who is beloved than one who is feared. Love is preserved by the link of obligations, which owing to the baseness of men is broken at every opportunity for their advantage; but fear preserves you by dread of punishment which never fails."

One cannot buy friends or loyalty. True friendship springs from generosity of spirit and nobleness of mind and friendship encompasses the ability for friends to disagree and still to respect each other. "Because he [the Prince] can endure very well being feared whilst he is not hated which will always be as long as he abstains from the property of his citizens and subjects and from their women."

Good employers must see to it that respect is practiced among their employees, and strive to make their businesses into grander things than just vehicles for making money. Business must be conducted with honor and efficiency. Fairness must be maintained at all levels in a business.

In the event of unfairness at lower levels, by employees obliging or not, the blame will always fall at the door of the employer, no matter how amiable that employer may believe him- or herself to be. The truly successful prince, or employer, needs more than just ability: the employer needs the reputation for exercising revenge. "Then it is quite necessary for him to disregard the reputation of cruelty, for without it he would never hold his army united or disposed to its duties." In effect, clement generals do not control tough fighting forces. Such forces are held together by iron discipline, and the reputation for cruelty can be an advantage when controlling a large number of employees. The right reputation is a most useful tool in business.

The good and successful employer must manage with certainty, a certainty that instructions will be obeyed, and a certainty that those instructions are the right instructions. In the world of business there must be no room for doubt, each problem must be approached with the attitude of no compromise. Never must employee or opponent be aware that you have a fall-back position prepared, though this will in all probability be the case. Certainty is the style that the employer must communicate to all employees.

When discussing dismissals, Machiavelli writes, "He must do it on proper justification and proper cause." However, life is seldom as straightforward as this and humans are devious in the extreme. Great caution must be taken with dismissals, especially when dealing with individuals who are both stupid and shrewd at the same time—a more common occurrence than would at first seem to be the case. Such individuals again are among the most dangerous with whom you will have to contend.

Hannibal, had his elephants died in the snow of the Alps and his soldiers faced starvation and his army suffered defeat, would have exhibited entirely different characteristics and played rather a different role in Machiavelli's great work, *The Prince*. Machiavelli quite rightly points out that the sort of reputation required to control an empire or great business is often not the sort of reputation much admired by those who contribute their words to newspapers. "And short-sighted writers admire his [Hannibal's] deeds from one point of view and from another condemn the principal cause of them." This is why many of those who succeed in business hire men and women skilled in presenting facts or words that seem to be facts in a way convenient to their aims and ambitions. What they present is more often than not far from the truth, but it is the perceived truth and this is what matters.

Machiavelli wrote: "Scipio, that most excellent man, not only of his own times but within the memory of man, against whom, nevertheless his army rebelled in Spain; this arose from nothing but his too great forbearance, which gave his soldiers more licence than is consistent with military discipline. For this he was upbraided in the Senate by Fabius Maximus, and called the Corrupter of the Roman Soldiery. The Locrians were laid waste by a legate of Scipio, yet they were not avenged by him, nor was the insolence of the legate punished, owing entirely to his easy nature." Happily, for Scipio, he was removed from command by the Senate. Had he continued in command, Machiavelli is of the opinion that his amiable nature "would have destroyed in time the fame and the glory of Scipio." Incidentally, at this point Machiavelli points out one of life's great truths: "There were many men who knew much better how not to err than to correct the errors of others." This point must not be forgotten either when you hire new employees or promote existing employees to positions of greater importance.

The average employee wants job security, a good wage, little responsibility and a good pension at the end of a life's work, but does not wish to be deeply involved in how these benefits are achieved. Nor does that employee want the responsibility for achieving these ends or the blame from fellow employees for failing to achieve them. The average employee does, however, require to be treated fairly and with respect. It is not for the average employee that Machiavelli wrote *The Prince* or indeed for whom I have penned this volume. This work is a guide for those who would, with courage and energy, rise above their fellow humans, and for those who, having carefully calculated all options, are prepared to take the risks necessary to succeed. Such an employee wishes to take on responsibility, earn a large wage and rise in the hierarchy of a business. Though awkward and argumentative, such a person is the material that is needed for promotion, and if not promoted and not rewarded, becomes a danger to the business. Such a person is often treated with suspicion and indeed fear. The business that would reject this person will be an ideal target when that person becomes a predator.

As discussed, never forget "the little people" in a business, for "the little people" have great power. By "little people" I mean telephonists, receptionists, secretaries and their kind. Friendship with those who do apparently menial jobs will make your life so much easier. Gain their loyalty and give loyalty to them in return. Should you be in a position with the power to direct, always remember that the will of these little people will affect how facts are presented to you. With their cooperation life is much easier and news will travel swiftly to your ear. Without their cooperation life will become harder and news will never reach you.

A company cannot be managed to its full potential unless the one who directs that company has allies in other businesses. Equally, to rise in a business, allies at all levels are necessary. Remember well that the leader who is deserted by old allies is in terrible danger, and that person had better find new allies without delay before it is too late. In all matters to do with the choice of executives, directors, the workforce and the management of the company, it is vital that your employees believe what you say and they believe that you will do what you say. As for being feared or not, Machiavelli advises, "Returning to the question of being feared or loved, I have come to the conclusion that men loving according to their own will and fearing according to that of the Prince, the wise Prince should establish himself on that which is in his own control and not in that of others." The wise prince or person who controls companies seldom uses fear as a tool of management. However, such a person must understand that if matters are not carried out as expected fear can be invaluable.

14

On the Secretaries Who Accompany the Prince.

THE POWER OF THE EMPLOYEE

The choice of ministers is a task of no little importance for a Prince. Whether they are good or not depends upon the prudence of the Prince.

Employees are of paramount importance. Their employer must have confidence that they will use the words that he would have them use rather than have them express their own preferences and prejudices. The employees, equally, must have confidence that their employer will back them in what they say. Employers who go back on the words of their employees will not be able to find employees of the quality needed to achieve true success. It is an important fact that the fate of the largest businesses lies in the hands of their most junior employee. An upset customer can lose a company vast amounts of business, and due to rudeness or insolence terminate a call that might have brought great profit. In the world of hotels the quality of service changed when elevator attendants were replaced by automatic elevators. This change, although a physical change, was reflected in

the mental attitude of all who work in hotels to their customers. The bond of friendship between elevator attendant
and the customers has never been replaced. There is no sub-
stitute for human contact: a disembodied voice is not at all
the same as a telephonist. As these changes become the
norm, the customers are distanced from the supplier, so
finding it easier to take their custom elsewhere. The returns
from increased efficiency by the use of machines in contact
with the customer must be carefully weighed against the
dangers.

Those engaged in business have cause to worry about
many things, but of all the choices that they have to make by
far the most important is choice of the staff that they employ. Worry continuously about your staff, for you are truly
in their power. "The first opinion which one forms of a
Prince and of his understanding is by observing the men he
has around him; and when they are capable and faithful, he
may always be considered wise, because he has known how
to recognize the capable and to keep them faithful." In every
man and woman there lies the capacity to achieve great
deeds in one field or another, but this does not mean that
they will achieve great deeds in all fields, or even in the field
at which they believe they excel. The skill of the management of mankind is to choose carefully the opportunities
given to employees and to watch how those employees re-
spond to opportunity. Beware most of all of over-promoting
an employee. Balance this danger with the fact that it is
possibility—the possibility of success or the possibility of
promotion—that motivates people. Never remove the possibility of employees improving their positions.

Employees left for a long time in the same job, not because they are unsuitable for promotion, rather because
they do that job well, will become stale and slap-happy, and
if they have energy to spare, that energy will be employed

elsewhere—perhaps in treachery or plotting. An employer should watch carefully the employees who find their job too easy, as well as those who find their job too hard. Always be suspicious of employees who work too hard, never taking a holiday, for such people may have something to hide and fear that all will be discovered while they are on holiday. In Machiavelli's words, "But when they are otherwise [found unsatisfactory] one cannot form a good opinion of him [the employer or Prince], for the prime error which he made was in choosing them." It is important to emphasize that the same principle applies to your friends—by your friends, so shall you be known. Sometimes judgments are unfair and on most occasions you will believe them to be unfair. Most likely you will stick with your friends, despite what others believe of them. While such actions are laudable in one respect, they are folly in another; if others believe your friends to be second-rate, so they believe you to be second-rate. There is no way around this other than to prove your critics wrong in the matter of yourself. It is important to note, however, that such critics may be justified in their opinion for their views are not cluttered by the emotion of friendship.

Machiavelli writes, "Because there are three classes of intellects: one which comprehends by itself [Princes or employers]; another which appreciates what others comprehend [the servant or employees of quality]; and a third which neither comprehends by itself nor by the showing of others [the employee who is relegated to menial tasks]." Machiavelli regards the last category of person as useless. Here he is mistaken, for these people, although they may not be much use at the tasks they have been given, may be extremely useful in other respects—in seeking out information, for instance. Being, by and large, simple people, they have simple ideas and come to simple conclusions. Never should an employer injure these people, for such is their or-

dinariness that they are often unobserved as they go about
their duties, noting and listening. Always remember when
employing staff that able people like to be in charge of someone else. Staff tend to want more staff. When new staff arrive and reduce the numbers of the staff in their department,
that reduction is seldom permanent, the last state of that office being greater than its first. Only the employer can au-
thorize the numbers employed, and, above a certain level,
only an employer can personally handle dismissals and the
employee should not expect otherwise.

"But to enable a Prince to form an opinion of his Servant, there is one test which never fails; when you see the
servant thinking more of his own interest than of yours and
seeking invariably his own profit in everything, such a man
will never make a good Servant [employee], nor will you
ever be able to trust him." The amiable employer made a
mistake on all three accounts. First, the obliging employee
talked of sharing profits, a not unusual request, and the amiable employer believed that this man meant to share when,
in fact, he intended to take the whole. Second, the obliging
employee sought power, and the amiable employer believed
that this man sought power the better to run the amiable
employer's business, when in fact the man sought power for
power's sake. Thirdly, the obliging employee wanted, above
all else, prestige. Seeing his amiable employer had prestige,
the obliging servant believed that he only had to instruct
prestige to be given to him and that prestige was then his.
He did not realize that prestige is like the skins of nacre on
a pearl, each skin acquired after years of friction and irrita-
tion with pieces of grit, years of rolling with the tides and
adverse waves.

The obliging employee had, because it suited him, given up
all respect for the amiable employer and believing him to be

weak, decided to steal these attributes, along with his employer's business — attributes that all should remember cannot be stolen, for they can only be earned. Had the obliging employee been a man of intellect and had he read the works of our incomparable genius, Machiavelli, he would have informed himself of the following words: "He who has the state of another in his hands, ought never to think of himself, but always of his Prince, and never pay any attention to matters in which his Prince is not concerned." This is invaluable advice both for those who work in a business and for those who run a business on behalf of shareholders. Those who own a business can do as they like, given only the restraints of the law and the banks who finance them, but should also take into account obligations towards those who work for them.

Machiavelli accepts the power of employees and even an employer's obligation to employees, not for moral reasons, rather for reasons of practicality. "To keep his servant honest, the Prince ought to study him, honouring him, enriching him, doing him kindness, sharing with him the honours and cares, at the same time let him see that he cannot stand alone." This is admirable advice that would have stood the amiable employer in good stead. However, all the actions of the amiable employer conspired to convince the obliging employee that he was not only totally capable of standing on his own, but would make a better job of running the company than his amiable employer. It was a classic case, put succinctly by Sir Winston Churchill, who was of the opinion that if he could buy a man at his estimate of the man's worth, and sell him at the man's own estimate of his worth, he would make a considerable profit. With the amiable employer and the obliging employee, you have two people closely associated, each going out of their way to get along together and neither having the first inkling of the aims and ambitions of the other. "So that many honours may not make him desire more, many riches make him wish for more." This is exactly what happens in my apologue of the amiable employer, the able lieutenant and the obliging employee. The honor and rewards paid to the obliging employee only gave him an irresistible taste for more, "And that many cares may make him dread changes." Should your employees have become too powerful, or even corrupt, the action that they dread most is change. This dread is perhaps the most expensive effect of their conceit or corruption, as they will fight like veritable tigers to avoid change, for when change comes, they are exposed for what they are. So in this sad apologue change had to come: the obliging employee had to leave the employ of the company, the amiable employer had to retire from the fray and the able lieutenant, watching from afar, saw how the kingdom and the spoils thereof could have been his own, if only he had displayed courage at a moment of crisis.

Always remember that while there will be many dire problems there is seldom a crisis. Just as when measuring a person's wealth, you should listen to the figure you are told, then believe half of a half of a half of that figure to be nearer the truth, so it is in a crisis, the danger is in truth half of the half of the predictions that you are given. As for the urgent need to deal with this matter, a crisis does not benefit from urgency—never sign documents in a hurry, always delay. Let a crisis, like a fever, run its course.

So it was that the able lieutenant lost, the obliging employee lost and the amiable employer lost—the reason for failure lying in the fact that each of them pursued their self-interest, rather than devoting themselves to the improvement of the business where they were employed. The pursuit of your own interests to the detriment of your responsibilities is just another example of greed.

So much power have employees that they can, with their folly, destroy the greatest of companies. "When, therefore, Servants, and Princes towards servants are thus disposed, they can trust each other, but when it is otherwise, the end will always be disastrous for either one or the other." Employers must choose wisely their employees, remembering the power they have and knowing that they have the capability to destroy.

15

On Ecclesiastical Principalities.

DEALING WITH THE ESTABLISHMENT

Now it only remains for us to discuss ecclesiastical principalities, which present difficulties prior to being possessed. For they are acquired either through personal ability or fortune and held on to without the help of either, because they are sustained by the ancient rules and institutions of the Church which have been of such strength and of such a type that they keep their Princes in power irrespective of how they act and live.

Machiavelli, with these words, has touched on the essential aspects of the "Establishment," for the Establishment extends far beyond the boundaries of business into political, social and often religious life. Machiavelli continues: "These Princes alone have states [businesses] and do not defend them. They have subjects [employees] and do not rule them; and the states, although unguarded, are not taken from them, and the subjects, although not ruled do not care, and they have neither the desire nor the ability to alienate themselves. Such principalities only are secure and happy. But being upheld by powers to which the human [who is not a member of the Establishment] cannot reach."

111

❊   ❊   ❊

The Establishment is an enigma: a group of people, mostly of similar backgrounds brought together by self-interest and kept together by tradition. Their businesses do not have to be efficient, for they are sustained by one another. Their employees do not have to be energetic, for they remain in office largely out of habit. They continue to do their work much as they have always done their work and they never rock the boat. In return, they have secure employment, because their employer will never get rid of them, and they know that the businesses that they work for are safe from attack or bankruptcy. If one member of the Establishment is attacked, the others will rally to support that member. However, taking over and owning a business that is of the Establishment does not by any means ensure that the new owner becomes a member of that Establishment. For, in truth, all that this person owns is a business that was formerly owned by a member of the Establishment. The nature of those who would climb to success from creating their own wealth will inevitably lead them to make changes to any business that they acquire. In doing so they will become the enemies of the Establishment, rather than part of that Establishment. In modern times, the Establishment in some countries is under attack and there have been casualties — businesses that the Establishment has decided not to save. The Establishment will never hesitate to make a sacrifice in order to save itself.

Do not imagine that the Establishment only operates in countries of a particular nature of politics, for the Establishment thrives under dictators and democracies, under communism and under capitalism. The Establishment has an order to its existence, an order that is not written down and seldom spoken about, an order passed from generation to generation, by instinct as much as in any other way.

The Establishment thrives on order but is flexible in how that order is maintained. The Establishment will destroy those who disrupt order and frustrate those who threaten order. The membership of the Establishment changes over the years, but its aims and ambitions never alter. The desire to rule in its own interest is the Establishment's aim and in return it gives the citizens of the country in which it operates an orderly society, which, by habit, they have come to expect. These citizens do not bother to consider whether this Establishment is operating in their best interests or not, for they would far rather have order than anarchy. Anarchy is anathema to the Establishment, and while an Establishment exists, anarchy does not prosper.

The Establishment spans the main political parties and can do business with whichever of these parties is in power. Should a political philosophy uncongenial to the Establishment threaten to take power, the Establishment will unite in order to frustrate its intentions.

Success does not secure an entry to the Establishment; rather, success has exactly the reverse effect. The Establishment has a contempt for success, its members having never needed success to be part of the Establishment. Too little wealth is not a bar to being a member of the Establishment, for a person or business may hold that position by tradition, long after success and wealth have gone. Too much wealth, on the other hand, is often a bar to membership of the Establishment, for the Establishment is not immune to human instincts such as jealousy and fear.

Trifle with the Establishment and you will, without doubt, fail—even as you triumph. Do not, for one moment, believe that the Establishment operates in splendid isolation, for this is far from the case. Outsiders may trade with the Establishment. In fact, the Establishment usually trades with outsiders and often with great success. The Establishment has its friends, and rewards them well. It often uses outsiders to fulfill its strategies and, over a period of years, forms a close relationship with these organizations and their proprietors. There remains, however, the Rubicon that cannot be crossed, for those who trade with the Establishment and those who are its tools can never join the Establishment. "These potentates had two principal anxieties; the one that no foreigner should enter Italy under arms; the other that none of themselves should seize more territory." The Establishment thrives in a balanced society, and its aim is to see that the society that it thrives within stays balanced.

The Establishment is a balance of factions who often squabble. Colleagues, however, see to it that a balance of power is maintained, for as Machiavelli writes, "If so to speak one Pope should almost destroy the Colonnesi; another would rise hostile to the Orsini, who would support their opponents, and yet would not have time to ruin the Orsini." Machiavelli, in this paragraph, catches the principle of the Establishment. No one joins and the pecking order of the existing members is maintained. The Establishment is a fragile thing, not unlike an egg, hard from the outside, easily broken from within. When broken it is smashed utterly and, like Humpty Dumpty, it is incapable of being put back together again.

The Establishment has among its members those skilled in cunning and often they will tempt those that they seek to profit from by offering these others the chance to become members of the Establishment. Forget such temptations and remove them from your mind, for those who offer them have no franchise to make such offers and they make these offers only out of self-interest, with little intention of delivering the promised prize. Do not imagine that all members of the Establishment are honest, wealthy or straightforward in their dealings and do not fall into the trap of being impressed by dealing with the Establishment. Judge every deal astutely on its own merits, for the Establishment offers no easy prizes. Charitable giving is not a way into the Establishment, but is expected of those who wish to do business with the Establishment. Do not be tempted into such excessive charitable giving. Charitable giving must be conducted from the heart and must not be conducted at a level that may endanger your business. The Establishment will take your money and you will receive little more than cursory thanks. The Establishment thrives on using other people, and is well practiced in that art.

Machiavelli tells of Pope Julius: "All these enterprises prospered with him, and so much the more to his credit inasmuch as he did everything to strengthen the Church [the Establishment of sixteenth-century Italy] and not any private person." Much of Pope Julius's success is attributed by Machiavelli to his refusal to allow that Establishment to splinter into rival groups, each with its own leaders. I quote, "And although there were among them some mind to make disturbance, nevertheless he [Pope Julius] held two things firm. The one, the greatness of the Church with which he terrified them [all who would disrupt order]; and the other, not allowing them to have their own Cardinals [leaders of rival Establishments] who caused disorder amongst them. For whenever these factions have their own Cardinals, they do not remain quiet for long, because Cardinals foster the factions in Rome and out of it, and the Barons are compelled to support them and thus from the ambitions of prelates arise disorder and tumult among the Barons."

Order is paramount in the survival of the Establishment and the Establishment knows this well and will go to endless trouble to maintain order, for the Establishment is an idea—an idea with a series of servants, but without a prince and therefore fragile. Each member of the Establishment is its servant, dedicated to the protection and promotion of the Establishment.

Those who seek success in a business created by their own hand do not ignore the existence of the Establishment. However, do not let the Establishment blind you to your own purpose. Do not seek favors from the Establishment, nor tread on the Establishment's toes. And, in particular, do not bother aspiring to a place in the Establishment, for such aspirations will only waste energy that could be better used to conduct your business. All the time that you struggle to join their ranks, the Establishment will chuckle with mirth, mocking your efforts as they believe you to be a fool. Far better to treat the Establishment distantly, having only a commercial relationship with these people, asking no favors, and giving no favors, unless, of course, those favors happen to be to your own commercial advantage.

16

How a Prince Should Act Concerning Military Affairs.

THE NEED FOR TOTAL DEDICATION

A Prince, therefore, should have no concern, no thought, or pursue any other art besides the art of war, its organization and instruction.

If the person in charge of a business's affairs is well versed in how to take over the control of another business, it stands to reason that such a person will be well versed in how to stop another taking over the business. Machiavelli continues, "For this is the sole Art that belongs to him who rules, and it is of such force that it not only upholds those who are born Princes, but it often enables men to rise from a private station to that rank." There is nothing more important than to learn your trade, for the person who attends business, to the exclusion of all else, will, in the end, by dedication, succeed. The person who has other priorities in life may well succeed, but only by natural talent, and such a person's undertakings will always be at risk. "And on the contrary, it is seen that when Princes have thought more of ease than of arms, they have lost their states and the first cause of your losing it, is to neglect this Art; and what enables you to acquire a state is to be a Master of the Art."

Machiavelli quotes several examples of how great principalities [businesses] are lost by neglect and idleness or won by diligence and attention to the art of war [or business]. There is no more admirable person than the self-made man or woman. These people have seen hard times and understand well the dedication needed to build and control a business. A truly self-made person is one who educated him- or herself while rising in the ranks of life, not one who has taken a small family business and made it larger, or whose family has provided an education. A person who truly started a business and came to success through quickness of mind and dedication of soul is rare indeed.

A self-made person who hands over his or her business to heirs ensures they have been prepared to inherit such a business. These children succeed because that is their destiny and they have been well taught the art of business by the best teacher. Their children, however, are a different matter. For them the business that they inherit prejudges the nature of their careers. Often they resent this, and while happy to enjoy the benefits of wealth, they find this great wealth a burden — one, however, that most of them are quite willing to bear. Such grandchildren may be highly intelligent and are often extremely well educated and may not be lazy or idle. Indeed, although they often work hard, that work is seldom at preserving the business of their grandparent. They more often than not have neither the desire nor the dedication to succeed in business, and while there are examples of businesses run by the later generations, these businesses are poor things by comparison with the original. The families who run them, being large, have from time to time produced able managers, where the rest of the family has the wit to allow the able manager who is their relative to manage, there is a chance of success. When relatives insist on managing collectively, there can only be failure. The irony of this whole situation is that failure, in the form of the disposal of their business, is what these relatives often seek, for only in this way can they lay their hands on money, an event that these feckless descendants regard as a triumph.

It is not in the nature of people who share control of a business equally to recognize the superior ability of one of their number. Nor is it their nature to allow a person of a superior ability the freedom to make them all successful, for generosity of spirit is the rarest of all emotions. Without the freedom that the founder of the business enjoyed, the relative of superior ability cannot perform. Machiavelli states that "it is not reasonable that he who is armed [well-informed] should yield obedience willingly to him who is unarmed [ill-informed]." Here lies the problem, for the well-informed person will sooner or later tire of this situation and look elsewhere for satisfaction, while the ill-informed person has already taken to other pursuits while still engaged in running the business. It is the ill-informed relatives who bring down the business that has been inherited, even if the well-informed relatives remain and work diligently for the general good of the family. These businesses are almost impossible to defend against attack and the practiced attacker will enlist the aid of the well-informed relative to bring about the conquering of that person's family business. Conquering is not too heavy a word to use in this context, for that is what the takeover or even merger of a business is all about.

The amiable employer may well imagine that he and his business are secure, believing that "the unarmed man should be secure among armed servants." In this security, the amiable employer deceives himself, for he lays himself open to the treachery of the obliging employee and is not only in danger from an outside attack but also in terrible jeopardy from within. "Because there being in one the disdain [for the amiable employer] and in the other suspicion [of treachery in the employees], it is not possible to work together." Such is the atmosphere that the obliging employee seeks to foster as his plans fall into place to steal his master's business. Businesses that have been inherited may well seem secure because their shares are owned by a small, closely associated group. If that group should ever split, the dangers are great indeed. There are other dangers to the inherited business, apart from an attack on their shares, and the chief among these dangers occurs when business is bad, for then the banks who have lent money will demand changes, perhaps even the disposal of the business. Here, the proprietors are in grave danger from the obliging employee. As I have explained, such a person must be kept away from banks and bankers.

The amiable employer, under attack from without and sabotage from within, can do little to thwart the obliging employee at this stage, even if he is aware of the plots and plans against him. Machiavelli concludes, "A Prince who does not understand the art of war, over and above misfortunes already mentioned, cannot be respected by his soldiers, nor can he rely on them."

The contempt of your colleagues, especially those who work for you, is a terrible thing, and renders your whole undertaking vulnerable to whoever will take that business from you. A person who would engage in business should never, in Machiavelli's words, "have out of his thoughts this subject of war and in peace he should addict himself more to its exercise than in war. This he can do in two ways, one by action, the other by study. As regards action, he ought, above all things, to keep his men well organized and drilled, to follow incessantly the Chase, by which he accustoms his body to hardships, and learns something of the nature of localities."

I cannot stress too often that you should look after your health, for health is vital to success. Garibaldi, for instance, prepared his body and his mind for the conquest of the states that he formed into Italy by working on a sailing vessel that crossed oceans. His body became fit by physical exercise, and his mind remained pure because he was out of the reach of corruption. Toughen your body in order to be able to withstand long hours of work when involved in a takeover battle and toughen your mind so that there is no panic in your soul when adverse events occur. Train your mind to realize that events, while they may suddenly occur, take time to come to fruition.

Deal with adverse fortune logically, one event at a time, and never allow yourself to be panicked or rushed into actions that you may regret. The rhythm of battle is attack, withdraw, defend, attack. The person who first develops a rhythm will take the initiative and, most likely, win. Machiavelli also advises that a leader "learns to know his country." I interpret that as meaning, learn the nature of your industry. Do that, and you may be better able to spot the likelihood of attack from potential predators. Machiavelli continues, a leader is then "better able to undertake its [his country's] defence." In both attack and defense, it is capabilities that matter, not intentions. For if a predator has the intention of attacking your business, that attack will come to nothing if that predator does not have the capability to sustain such an attack. Do not waste time merely with those who intend to attack your company: also watch with care those with the capability for attack.

In the time of attack, employ specialists in the matter of defense, but being warned of the dangers that come from employing mercenaries and auxiliaries, allow each of them only a small view of your affairs. The defense must be coordinated by the employer — only the employer must know all the plans. Treachery, both accidental and planned, is rife at the time of battle. In the end, information will be the key to victory, but information without the courage to make use of that information is worthless. Machiavelli writes, "With a knowledge of the aspect of one country, one can easily arrive at a knowledge of others."

Machiavelli was chiefly concerned with the Italian states when he wrote *The Prince*. The modern person in business must be concerned with the whole world, as that world is only seconds away by virtue of communications. The businessperson must study the practices of other countries in order to use them in the defense of the business. A person in business must read widely and learn endlessly, and must dedicate his or her life to the job; it must be realized that this is the case before such a person embarks on a career in business.

To attain outstanding success, at home and during leisure hours, such a person must discuss business endlessly: it must be an obsession. Machiavelli writes of Philopoemen Prince of the Achaeans, who, "among other praises which writers bestowed on him, is commended because in time of peace he never had anything in mind but the rules of war; and when he was in the country with friends, he often stopped and reasoned with them." A clever leader will learn from conversations with others. You must always talk to your employees and divine their intentions, and furthermore have conversations with those in all walks of life, for you do not know what they will tell you that you can make use of, and what is more, neither do they. The truly cunning leader will have a dozen different plans for a dozen different eventualities. Such a leader will take care that small events are taken into account, for small events often have grand consequences; and will plan and counter-plan, but waste no time in plotting. This leader will be open with others or say nothing—for such a leader is not devious. However, the leader will not expect others to be open, for that is not in the nature of humans. The leader is always ready to learn and always ready to try a new tactic. This strategy is fixed by virtue of a philosophy formed in the leader's youth.

The finest defense against attack is to be well prepared and Machiavelli writes, "A wise Prince ought to observe some such rules, and never in peaceful times stand idle, but increase his resources with industry in such a way that they may be available to him in adversity, so that if fortune changes it may find him prepared to resist her blows."

So far in this chapter, I have dealt largely with the art of defending a company that is likely to be under attack. However, here follow a few tactics which bear some similarities to tactics discussed earlier. First, put the public perception of your business in order. Let the public have a high regard for your activities, then set about destroying any good perceptions they may have of your opponents. After this, show how your opponents will, if they should win, destroy a business that the public likes and replace it with a business that the public hates. Specialists can be employed to do this work. Rally the support of the public, customers and any pressure groups that you can recruit in winning over your shareholders. This will prove to be extremely valuable.

Confuse the issue, talk of other bids, try to destabilize your opponents, try to have their attack examined by the authorities and demonstrate that their bid for your business does not mean what it says. The predator must have up-to-date intelligence in order to muster an attack, while your only role is to defend and to destroy whatever arguments the predator may deploy. If you fear attack, remove the assets from the business and so engage these assets in a manner that prohibits their sale until some time in the distant future. By taking the value from a business you reduce the prize that your opponent will win in victory, and the predator must then consider if the battle is worthwhile. In business, as opposed to politics, opponents battle for profit, not for principle.

In extremis, search for a friendly bid, but bear in mind that no bid is friendly in the end. When a business has been taken over it may well seem the same, but that is an illusion. The business will become, with time, totally different. When threatened with a takeover bid, make a bid for another company.

Read the records of all previous takeovers, whether or not they bear any similarity to your situation. Machiavelli wrote, "But to exercise the intellect the Prince should read histories and study the actions of illustrious men to see how they have borne themselves in war."

But, beware: your opponents may have read the same books.

"To examine the cases of the victories and defeat so as to avoid the latter and imitate the former, above all do as an illustrious man did who took as an example one who had been praised and famous before him; and whose achievements and deeds he always kept in his mind, as it is said Alexander the Great imitated Achilles, Caesar, Alexander, Scipio Syrus." The thrust of Machiavelli's words are that history not only teaches best, but that history is worth repeating. The danger of repeating history is that your total plan can be perceived if by chance your enemy is as well-informed as you. History is both a guide and a teacher—like all teachers, history must not be copied, but used as a springboard for the formulation of new strategies.

In any contest it is the person with the inventive and imaginative mind who will win, provided, of course, that person has learned the history of the trade and used that as a basis for formulating ideas. All who would do otherwise are merely gamblers who cast dice at random and move their counters at a whim. Sometimes these sort of people can win, but more usually they lose. Instinct, while an invaluable and indispensable ingredient of success, is not enough on its own: success is far more complicated.

17

Whether Princes Should Keep Their Word.

THE USE OF CRAFTINESS

Everyone understands how laudable it is for a Prince to keep his word and live with integrity and not cunning. Nonetheless, experience shows that nowadays those Princes who have accomplished great things have had little respect for keeping their word and have known how to confuse men's minds with cunning. In the end they have overcome those who have preferred honesty.

These words of Machiavelli have a ring of truth about them. However, the person who lies to achieve his or her ends will, in time, be found out and such achievements exposed as frauds. Those who are already powerful may well get away with their lies, or at least believe that they got away with those lies; in truth, however, liars only invite the lies of others, and there is no honor in their success and their failure is held in contempt by all. Through their lies, these people will create great enemies—people do not care to be deceived nor do they care to be tricked.

The lies of tricksters will fester in the minds of their victims. Should the trickster prosper by deceit and one day become powerful, then that trickster will become the victim of those to whom lies have been told. At the moment of the trickster's greatest triumph, the victim will expose the trick-

127

ster as a fraud. Do not forget that the ones who would rise by the use of lies live with those lies, always waiting for another to use those lies to pull them down. Machiavelli writes not of liars or their lies in this passage. He refers to craft and dangers of dealing with a crafty individual. There is a great difference between the use of craft, or even cunning, and the straightforward lie.

The truly cunning individual has a contempt for lies and deceit. Such a person has no need for such crude weapons and will always be able to overcome the liar and the deceitful individual. Machiavelli continues, "You must know there are two ways of contesting [conducting your business], the one by the law, the other by force; the first method is proper to men, the second to beasts; but because the first is frequently not sufficient, it is necessary to have recourse to the second." Both talents are found in varying degrees in the same individual, but it is the circumstance which will dictate the method and the instinct that is used.

When events of life run in your favor, then it is easy to behave with honor. When events run against you, there will come a point at which there is no alternative left other than the use of deceit. Deceit is the currency of failure. Take the case of the obliging employee, he was both cunning and deceitful, but in the event his cunning was exposed by his deceit. Had he the courage to only deal in cunning, then without doubt he would have managed to steal the business of the amiable employer. However, the obliging employee was greedy, he was impatient and he did not trust in his own talents. There was only a small deceit at first, but with time the obliging employee's deceits became bolder and the amiable employer, trusting the obliging employee, did nothing to rebut these deceits. The cunning of the obliging employee had changed from craft to treachery and deceit and then to downright dishonesty. The irony of the situation was that neither the amiable employer nor the obliging employee noticed what was happening. Only by fate and a change of circumstance will the deceit and lies of the obliging employee be exposed.

Machiavelli writes, "Therefore it is necessary for a Prince to understand how to avail himself of the beast and the man." People who would rise in business must understand both cunning and deceit, so that they may use cunning themselves and so that they may recognize deceit when it is used against them. Machiavelli writes the following words in what is possibly the most controversial passage in the whole of his work *The Prince*. "So it is necessary for a Prince to know how to make use of both natures, and that one without the other is not durable." In the matter of success achieved by deceit, Machiavelli writes using his analogy with animals, "A Prince therefore being compelled knowingly to adopt the beast, ought to choose the fox and the lion, because the lion cannot defend himself against snares and the fox cannot defend himself against wolves. Therefore it is necessary to be a fox to discover the snares and a lion to terrify the wolves. Those who rely simply on the lion do not understand what they are about."

As for the keeping of one's faith: "Therefore a wise lord cannot, nor ought he to, keep faith when such observances may be turned against him, and when the reasons that caused him to pledge it exist no longer." The precept that Machiavelli outlines in a passage that denies principle is that if you are lied to, you should lie back. If you are tricked into an agreement, then it is as if you have not made that agreement. Machiavelli continues, "If men were entirely good, this precept would not hold [there would in those circumstances be no need for such a precept] but because they are bad, and will not keep faith with you, you are not bound to observe it with them." Remember always when you conduct your affairs, that those whom you deal with will always find a way of convincing themselves that you have cheated them, if that is convenient to them, in order to avoid agreements made with you. That instinct is as true today as it was in the fifteenth century when Machiavelli wrote, "Nor will there ever be wanting to a Prince legitimate reasons to excuse his nonobservance." He goes on: "Of this endless modern [fifteenth-century] examples could be given, showing how many treaties and engagements have been made void and of no effect through the faithlessness of Princes." Had Machiavelli been writing today, his words would have been no different. He concludes, "He who has known best how to employ the fox has succeeded best." The whole thrust of Machiavelli's work is a realistic if cynical appreciation of the human character, understanding both its light and dark side. He continues this passage: "But it is necessary to know well how to disguise this characteristic and to be a great pretender and dissembler; and men are so simple and so subject to present necessities that he who seeks to deceive will always find someone who will allow himself to be deceived." It was thus between the obliging employee and his amiable employer.

Out of deceit and fraud comes only emptiness, especially in success. Machiavelli highlights the narrow line which runs between honesty and dishonesty. With cunning and craft, however, there is no need for dishonesty. Machiavelli writes, "Therefore it is unnecessary for a Prince to have all the good qualities I have enumerated, but it is very necessary to appear to have them. And I shall dare to say this also, that to have them and always observe them is injurious; and that to appear to have them is useful; to appear merciful, faithful, humane, religious, upright, and to be so but with a mind so framed that should you require not to be so, you may be able and know how to change to the opposite."

In truth an employer must be a mixture of characters, and the quality of the employer's own judgment is discovered when the employer selects which of these characters will be used in any particular situation. When Machiavelli wrote these words there was a huge outcry, for his text appeared to lack morality and to concentrate only on the art of winning. With the exception of this chapter, his words are as useful today as in his own age. Technology has changed much at the end of the twentieth century and it is no longer possible to guarantee apparent success through lies and deceit. What is more, the laws of our age are draconian in their revenge on those who deceive and are caught. The balance of risk and reward has changed, and it has changed dramatically against those who would commit corporate crime or attempt to deceive others through manufacturing a false image of their company.

The cunning truth is now more efficacious than the lie or deceit. Learn about lies but do not risk using them, for the world abounds with lawyers and laws who watch for those lies. In the hands of a truly imaginative person, where deceit becomes cunning, it can be used with impunity and without fear of the new laws. Machiavelli continues, "You have to understand this, that a Prince, especially a new one, cannot observe all those things for which men are esteemed, being often forced, in order to maintain the State to act contrary to fidelity, friendship, humanity and religion." He points out that at its highest level, loyalty and integrity are all subject to a greater truth, necessity, and thence the well-being of the state, which overrides all else.

At a level more akin to everyday life, Machiavelli means that in starting to rule a state (or a business) the options to be honest or good are somewhat limited. If you would succeed with honor and circumstances are such that you cannot, give up; for not all people are meant to lead and if you must deceive and lie to succeed, you are among those who do not have this destiny. Keep faith always with your employees, keep faith with your customers and above all keep faith with yourself, and if success does not find you, then at least you have honor, and one day perhaps events will run in your favor. Apart from the moral reasons, there are strong practical reasons why an employee should keep faith with an employer and vice versa. Without trust there will always be discontent in your workforce and with discontent comes absenteeism and lack of production, so defeating the whole point of business.

As for customers, you should treat them fairly at all times. If a customer cheats you, do not imagine that there is any advantage in trying to cheat the customer in return. It would be far better to avoid such a customer, for that customer will always cause you loss. Send the customer away with kind words and a recommendation to your greatest rival. By doing so in your most cunning manner, your rival will have the idea that he has stolen your customer, when in fact your rival steals only a great liability.

Machiavelli is hesitant to judge: "The actions of all men and especially Princes [chairpersons] which it is not prudent to challenge, one judges by the results." The important point to remember here is that, while it is all very well to judge a person by his or her actions and degree of success, this will only be an accurate judgment if based on fact not on what others would have you believe as fact. In Machiavelli's words, "Everyone sees what you appear to be, few really know what you are." Indeed, you may not truly know what you are yourself at the beginning of your career and by the end of it may very well have deceived yourself into believing that you are something entirely different from the reality. It is often this self-fantasy that gives people the courage and the energy that they need to succeed, striving hard to make their fantasy turn into their reality. Sometimes this works, but more often than not, it fails. Easy as it is to dream, it is far harder to fulfill those dreams.

Always in business appear to be consistent and demonstrate consistency by wearing the same style of clothes, dining at the same restaurants, keeping the same staff around you. Change direction when it is necessary, while indicating that you hold to your original course. Remember that this tactic is most useful when managing people, for they like to know what their situation is and fear change. The stance of a manager is that of protector, reassuring employees that while change is the natural order of things, their welfare and futures will be taken into consideration. There should be no doubt, however, that a person who succeeds by breaking faith and using deceit will sometimes go unpunished with no one aware of the perfidy. "One Prince of the present time, whom it is not well to name, never preaches anything else but peace and good faith, and to both he is most hostile, and either, if he had kept it, would have deprived him of reputation and Kingdom many a time." This prince, Ferdinand of Aragon, was well known to all who read Machiavelli's words. Machiavelli made sure that Ferdinand paid a lasting price for his lies and treachery, and exacted this price in his writing by destroying Ferdinand's reputation for honor.

When the pursuit of money changes to the pursuit of revenge, you are in grave danger. If for any reason the market should change, you may well lose both your money and the ability to exact revenge. Adversity is there to keep your pride in check and to remind you from time to time of the true dangers than can flow from the risks that you take. Adversity also reminds you of the difference between earning prestige and buying prestige, for only true prestige will remain in times of adversity. When times are good, put money and goodwill into your business. But do both things quietly, the one by keeping financial reserves and the other by improving facilities for those who work for you and helping the community among whom you work. Never take the view that conditions are good enough for today—always make sure that they are good enough for tomorrow. Always look to the future and never waste time worrying about the opportunities that you have lost, learn from them and move on.

Finally, let no bitterness enter your life from missed opportunities or adverse luck. Consider very carefully the mistakes that you have made and why you have made them, but waste no time on success that you have never had.

18

How the Strength of Every Principality Should be Measured.

FINANCE AND THE UNDERSTANDING OF MONEY

The cities of Germany are totally free, have little surrounding territory and obey the Emperor only when they want to. They do not fear him or any other neighbouring power, as they are fortified in such a way that everybody is aware that it would be a tedious and difficult exercise to vanquish them. For they all have well-placed walls and moats, all the artillery they need and enough food, drink, and fuel for a year housed in their public stores. In addition, they keep enough supplies under public control to be able to furnish the people with the means to ply their trades for a whole year without loss to the public purse. These are the life and soul of the city, and the means whereby the people can earn a living. They also consider military exercises important, and as a result have many provisions and institutions relating to their upkeep.

In order for commerce of any sort to function, it is necessary for buyers to believe that the goods they buy are worth more than the price put on them by the seller. At its most primitive, commerce works thus: one who sells cheeses decides that five cheeses are worth a large bundle of logs. The participants in this transaction, likely as not, will argue over the relative values of cheeses and logs, but the deal that they make is of no importance to the principle. The one who owns cheeses needs logs more than cheese. The logs have a particular value to the cheese seller who has no logs, and another value to the log seller, who has plenty of them. Were there to be a universal value set on the labors of employees or the goods that they produce, a value that never varied, a value the same to the one who buys as to the one who sells, and were all who traded to believe that their goods were of equal value, then commerce would come to a standstill, for all chance of making a profit would cease. It is an essential tenet of all commerce that one party believes their efforts to be of greater value than the efforts of another. It is because one set of people value a particular product at one figure, and another set of people value that product at a higher figure, that a profit is made, and likewise, were a third set of people to value the same product at less than the second set of people, a loss would be made. Those who would prosper in business must first grasp this principle, then they must realize that the view people take of the value of their labor alters from time to time as does the value employers set on the labors of their employees.

The value of any company is only worth what you can do with that company. Similarly, the same is true of a property. The price that you paid for either property or company has nothing to do with its true value, neither has the price that is asked for property or company. When looking at the value of a kiosk selling hot dogs in the center of Tokyo, some might say it is worth very little; others might say it is worth a fortune. It is actually worth no more than just the profit returned by selling hot dogs unless one were to suggest building an office building on the site of the kiosk; then the value would increase immeasurably. Those who will prosper must use imagination, then have the ability to turn imagination into reality. Great increases in the value of companies come only from the managerial skill of those who run them, and likewise, great decreases in the value of companies come only from the incompetence of those who run them.

In business the trick is to avoid having to sell when people believe your goods or services to be less valuable than you do. Thus, you should conduct your business affairs in the same way that Machiavelli reports that the cities of Germany conducted theirs, always from a position of strength. Life being as it is, those who would buy your goods and services can often sense the weakness of your position, or if you have in your employ an obliging employee who would ingratiate himself with others, those to whom you would sell may have privy information as to the weakness of your situation. Machiavelli writes, "It is necessary to consider another point in examining the true character of these principalities [businesses]. That is, whether a Prince has such power [financial resources] that in case of need he can support himself with his own resources, or whether he has always need of the assistance of others [usually banks]. To make this quite clear, I say that I consider those are able to support themselves by their own resources, who can, either by abundance of men or money, raise a sufficient army to join battle against anyone who comes to attack them." Machiavelli, pointing out the necessity of having cash in the bank in case a business falls on hard times when its product is no longer needed, also seems to make reference to what we would call a hostile takeover. However, a hostile takeover bid is more likely to occur if a company does have money in the bank and is successful (or has the potential for success) but, because of the vagaries of the market, is undervalued. So, I conclude that the right posture for a business to adopt is one of a sound financial base, carrying only the funds needed to run the business in hand. Importantly, however, it should have reserves that are held in other businesses ready for use in hard times. These reserves should be held in a different form so as not to be affected by the same hard times that have afflicted the primary business.

More businesses have been brought down by success than by failure. Their very success leads the management to borrow money in order to finance their expanding business, and excessive borrowing will almost inevitably lead to failure. One of the most important aspects of running a business is the understanding of money—not just a technical understanding, but a feel for how money comes and how money goes—and furthermore, a talent, which is called financing, for bridging the gap between the two. An employer must know how to raise money and how to use money. The management of people is of vital importance when running a business, but a talent to manage people without the corresponding talent for managing money is useless.

Beware of banks, as discussed, for banks will always lend you money when times are easy. In fact, they will positively encourage you to borrow from them: lending money is their business, and that is how they make their profits. To those who start out in business and are unfamiliar with bankers, these people seem to take the role of referee. They look at your accounts and give what appears to be an impartial view as to the success or otherwise of your business. If they say you are successful, then you are flattered and pleased, thus making an easy and willing victim for those who would sell you money, for that is what bankers do when they make a loan. If they tell you that your business is worthless, you are angry, depressed and you visit yet more bankers until you succeed in borrowing—and if times are good, you will find someone to lend money to you, even for the most crack-brained idea. In both instances, the person who would borrow money for the company regards the banker as one who understands business. This is the most terrible of errors, for a banker is a man or woman who understands banking, a very different matter from understanding business in general and your business in particular. Bankers are interested in only two matters: first, can your business service the interest that they charge on lending you money, and second, if all goes wrong, will there be enough money left to repay their debt?

These conclusions are the ones that will influence whether or not they will lend you money. In good times, bankers are not greatly interested in how their debt is repaid or even when, provided the assets of the business that they lend to are greater than the loan by a considerable margin. Coupled with these conclusions are other considerations, for instance, your record of success and, strangely, the record of success that your competitors enjoy. A failure to lend may have nothing to do with you or your business, rather it has to do with the failure of others in the same line of business. When times are hard, the bank's attitude will change: gone are the friendly bankers and in their stead are cold, hard strangers who are interested only in the return of their bank's funds, usually at once. Their only interest in keeping a business alive is primarily to recover those funds.

In these circumstances, it is greatly to your advantage to owe your banker large sums of money. For the larger the sum that you owe, the more considerate the banker will be, for after all it is the bank's money that is being considered. The record of the borrower in such a situation is of no account. It will be of no help if your company has banked with this bank for over one hundred years. Even a perfect record of repaying previous debts will be of no account. Under no circumstances ever give a personal guarantee to borrow money, or for that matter pledge your home. Banks do not behave fairly—fairness is just an image of a bank, but not the fact.

If your debt is small, they will, in all probability, put you into liquidation. If your debt is very large, they will engineer your affairs so that for years you work only for the bank, until you reach the moment when the value of your business is greater than the money that you owe them. At that point, despite all the hard work of paying off your debts, they will destroy both your business and, in all likelihood, you as well. A bank should not be blamed for such conduct—it is the very nature of their trade and those that would engage in business should know this.

As explored earlier, bankruptcy is the spur to capitalism and profit is capitalism's reward. Without the spur and the reward, capitalism cannot truly function and commerce dies. Bankruptcy, both corporate and personal, in America is regarded as just another failed business venture. It carries no social stigma and those who go bankrupt start again with alacrity. Banks in America are open to offers of stock in the company or purchase of the debt. A personal guarantee weakens your position when negotiating either of these. In Britain, bankruptcy is still a personal dishonor and banks are still rigid in their search for solutions to the situation of insolvent companies. American banks take a more enlightened attitude than the British, not out of kindness, rather because such an enlightened attitude is a more effective way of recovering funds.

Anyone who doubts the lack of a banker's ability to understand another man's business, ought to observe how the greatest bargains are those businesses bought from bankers. Anyone who doubts the ability of those who work in a business to know its true value, only has to observe the great profits made by businesses recently purchased by those who work in them. It is too easy a solution to suggest that these profits only arise because men and women work harder for themselves than they do for an employer.

Machiavelli continues with his theme of the need for strength: "And I consider those always to have need of others who cannot show themselves against the enemy in the field, but are forced to defend themselves by sheltering behind walls." Without financial strength a business must be passive. That business cannot go out into the market to acquire other businesses, it cannot grow and will fail or become victim to another. For passive businesses and those who run them, Machiavelli recommends, "One can say nothing except to encourage such Princes to provision and fortify their towns, and not on any account to defend the country." So often the advice given by outside experts and bank managers to those who run companies that find themselves in hard times is to sell off the subsidiaries and concentrate on the core business. This advice puts into reverse the whole strategy of diversification in order to spread risk and leaves a business vulnerable to the cold winds of fate. Machiavelli does, however, have some words of comfort for those in this position. "And whoever shall fortify his town well and shall have managed the other concerns of his subjects in the way stated above, and to be often repeated, will never be attacked without great caution, for men are always adverse to enterprises where difficulties can be seen, and it will be seen not to be an easy thing to attack one who has his town well fortified." That sort of business is unlikely to be taken over by a competitor. However, with a business under pressure from all sides, the wretched owner is most probably trying to sell that business in any case.

It is worth quoting again Machiavelli's words from the beginning of this chapter regarding well-defended cities:

"They always have the means of giving work to the community [the employees] in those labours that are the life and strength of the city [the business]." Thus, the continuity of employment offered by the well-financed business greatly reduces the cost of running that business, through savings made by the lack of need for hiring and training staff. Such employees will not be subject to self-interest, whereas in a business with failing finances the best employees will leave first.

Machiavelli further states, "That a powerful and courageous Prince will overcome all such difficulties by giving at one time hope to his subjects that the evil will not be for long, at another time fear of cruelty of the enemy, then preserving himself adroitly from those subjects who seem to him to be too bold." The latter can be compared with the untrustworthy, obliging employee, who would conspire to steal his employer's business.

It is a strange fact of business that an undertaking which finds itself in the most adverse of circumstances, on being acquired by another business of high repute and financial strength, will recover its former strength without the introduction of new funds or for that matter substantial changes to its management. This phenomenon is caused by the reaction to the truth and the perceived truth. In the same way that the company's apparent weakness was perceived by all and became the truth, so its strength, due now to being owned by a strong corporation, is perceived by everyone and becomes the truth. In fact, nothing has changed in the affairs of that company, only the way that its affairs are perceived.

The real truth of the matter is this: first, the business is short of money so it is in trouble and that is perceived to be the case. As a consequence, the value of that business's assets tumble and its situation is perceived to be worse. As a result of the perceived situation, the company's real situation becomes dire. A new proprietor takes over this troubled business, and because this proprietor is perceived to have large funds, the business is no longer seen to be in trouble. The assets of that business will now rise in value against the market trend, for they are no longer available to the market, and this new business is now, in reality, sound. Had the banks and the shareholders taken the same view of that troubled business, and stood behind the company, showing their support publicly, then there would have been no need for a new owner and both the banks and the shareholders would have prospered.

Machiavelli continues to write in a way that could well be applied to the plight of a business in trouble which fails to find a new owner of courage to save it and to those who depend upon it. "Further, the enemy would naturally on his arrival at once burn and ruin the country." The obliging employee who has behaved with perfidy throughout the piece is the enemy within a failing business, taking what can be taken while it is still available. The amiable employer is fully occupied elsewhere, first trying to save the business and then arranging for that business to fall into safe hands. Businesses have a life of their own, with both their own achievements and their own responsibilities, and the destruction of a business is a sad matter.

No business can survive, however large or small, if that business is without astute financial management. As discussed earlier, whether the employer who runs that business is a hard and careful employer or an amiable employer, there must be strong financial management. The appointment of a financial manager entails the giving over of immense power and there must be checks and balances put into place to counter that power. An employer must at all times be the one with ultimate control. To those of a creative and inventive turn of mind, a dedication to the financial affairs of a business may be uncongenial, but it would be immensely destructive not to maintain the ultimate control of the business's financial affairs. It is not enough for an employer to imagine that because an employee has been treated well, the employee will return such behavior. As Machiavelli points out, the opposite is often likely to be the case. "For it is the nature of men to be bound by the benefits they confer as much as by those they receive." In other words, when you look for help, look to those who have shown you help and friendship, rather than to those whom you have helped and befriended.

I have written at length about the evil habits of banks and how they behave in hard times. The truth of the matter is that good and bad instincts exist in all of mankind. It is the circumstances in which humans find themselves that decide whether those people behave well or badly. Furthermore, the attitude of humans as to how they will behave is colored by their view of the future. For instance, a person who expects to die will often behave well, for the future is uncertain. Equally, a person faced with the destruction of their family, their business and their way of life can be a person of great honor, and yet the circumstances are such that this person will behave dishonorably. It is easy for all of us, in varying degrees, to behave with honor in good circumstances; it is less easy when the circumstances are adverse.

Nevertheless, honor lies deep in the soul of the dishonorable as dishonor lies in the soul of the most honorable of humans; and so it is with banks. Remember this when you borrow money, and whomever you borrow that money from, never allow a situation to arise where they can behave dishonorably. I do not mean to give the impression that borrowing money is necessarily an evil, rather that, when you borrow money, you must have a strategy for that money's repayment. There must be a planned exit. Never imagine that money can be borrowed without risk. Money must be borrowed in business, but it should be borrowed with a blend of caution, courage and knowledge. The borrowing of money and the banks that lend money are both part of the great chain of commerce. Without banks and the facility to borrow money, commerce dies. Equally, do not imagine that banks are the only source of finance for a business, for providing equity is one of the roles of a shareholder, another is, from time to time, the providing of loans to finance a business in which they own shares. However, managers must remember that whether money is borrowed from a bank or a shareholder, each will judge the risks with little thought for your welfare, and each will ask a return.

19

On Generosity and Meanness.

CONTROLLING EXPENDITURE

**I maintain that it would be good to be considered
generous. Nevertheless, generosity, when used in such a
way as to gain you that reputation, will damage you.
Because if used virtuously and as it should be used, it is not
recognized, and you will not avoid the infamy of its
opposite. Therefore if you want to establish a name for
yourself as a generous person, you cannot afford to neglect
any kind of lavishness. A Prince who acts this way will soon
use up all his resources and will eventually, if he wishes to
maintain a name for being generous, be constrained to
impose extra taxes in addition to the normal levies, and be
rigorous and do all he can to acquire money.**

Thus Machiavelli writes of liberality and the dangers of
high living to impress others. The employer who would
have the reputation for liberality will, in effect, take too
much money out of the company and endanger the jobs and
livelihoods of the employees. "This will soon make him odious to his subjects and becoming poor he will be little valued by anyone." So Machiavelli warns the profligate
employer. However, this warning goes against the instincts
of mankind, for it is part of human nature for people to

want to be loved and they will sometimes risk all to achieve this object.

Men may wish to be loved for their generosity. Women are less prone to this failing for their self-esteem is higher than that of men and they prefer to be loved for the totality of themselves. The desire to acquire love is a danger that must be guarded against. Equally, glorying in a reputation for stinginess is also destructive. Actions must be taken only for the good of the corporation and not for the feeling of satisfaction that these actions give to the chairperson of that corporation. What is more, there must always be a reason for taking a particular line of action when running a corporation and that line of action must be explained to those who work for that corporation at all levels. The explaining of actions is a delicate matter, for those who plan the strategy of a corporation obviously will not wish to show their hand to competitors. Furthermore, it must already be understood by those who work for a corporation that an explanation is not an invitation to debate, but rather shows the thinking that has taken place in coming to a conclusion. The conclusion is also an instruction. Even when understanding the reasoning behind that line of action, employees may still not approve of it. This is, in truth, immaterial. The important result is that they will not be confused about what is happening — confusion is the enemy of productivity. A corporation must have clear lines of command and clear instructions from those who command. One rule must be that extravagance at any level in the corporation will not be tolerated. Money will not be spent unnecessarily on travel or entertainment. However, this sternness must not become an excuse for the cancellation of all travel and entertainment by those who are jealous because their own jobs do not involve such expenditure. Some corporations benefit greatly from executives traveling and entertaining, but other corporations have executives who invent excuses for travel and entertainment, for no better reason than that they enjoy these activities or even continue to do them out of habit, long after all benefit is past.

Money will, however, be spent on a new plant and this new plant will replace workers and the cost of production will fall. Money will be spent on promotion of the corporation's products and so sales will rise and workers will be hired. The company will prosper and workers' jobs will be secure. Salesmen will sell and they will be given the funds to conduct sales campaigns, be it for the entertainment of opinion-formers or through advertising. All this, however, must not be carried out on the basis of instinct. Sales campaigns, at whatever level, must be planned.

Funds that are not spent should be saved for use when an opportunity arises, so that strong corporations may be able to use their maximum force when they decide to fight. The harboring of funds for the day when your company is attacked, or wishes to attack others, is of vital importance. These carefully harbored funds will also see you through hard times. Machiavelli puts it thus: "If he is wise he ought not to fear the reputation of being mean, for in time he will come to be more considered than if liberal, seeing that with his economy, his revenues are enough, that he can defend himself against all attacks." Not fearing the reputation of being mean, however, is a very different matter from glorying in that reputation. Machiavelli warns, "A Prince should guard himself, above all things, against being despised and hated; liberality leads you to both. Therefore it is wiser to have a reputation for meanness which brings reproach without hatred, than to be compelled through seeking a reputation for liberality to incur a name for rapacity which begets reproach with hatred." Happily we have in modern times a word that cuts between meanness and generosity, and that word is efficiency—but efficiency is no use on its own, for efficiency must be administered by one with a generous spirit.

The motivation for economy in a corporation must only be efficiency, never conceit. Usually those companies where economy is the watchword are motivated by the conceit of those who run them. For example, an executive who flies for twelve hours and attends a meeting on return to the office the next day is a fool, as that person's employers are represented by half an executive. The employer who pays an executive a high salary and saves money on that person's travel, is a fool, for an executive who travels overnight uncomfortably will not perform well the next day. Instead, the only economy should be whether or not the executive should travel in the first place.

In business, there must always be a carefully considered reason for taking action, while in the generality of life, most actions are dictated by vanity. In business, it is never a case of whether a particular action costs too much, only of whether it is really necessary. Can the company afford for this action not to be taken? It is here that the heart of the matter lies. Having decided to take the action, it cannot be jeopardized by a tired executive or a delayed flight. Comfort and time are ingredients of success and are of far greater import than their cost. When the time comes for the success of a corporation to be judged, it would be far better for the management not to be regarded as mean or extravagant — such a view makes the great industrialist into a figure of ridicule. Better simply to be viewed as successful. Industrialists who succeed will always be highly regarded by those who do not know them. They have no need of the myths of generosity or meanness, these are only conceits and do not affect the love of a public unaware of their private habits. As for those who know them, these people are so few in number that they appear not to matter, and such industrialists

150

are so great in conceit that they do not care. Beware the industrialist who spends much time tending an image—it is only the public that matters to such people.

True generosity has little to do with saving money or giving extravagantly. It is generosity of the spirit. Giving of your own time is one example, as is listening to the words of another. It is also believing the best of people, giving them the benefit of the doubt and perhaps even being prepared to risk a friendship through saying honest words. Generosity of spirit is the quality of a leader among humans. The lending of money can turn a friend into an enemy; however, refusing to lend money can well do the same. Only when the act of giving or lending money is coupled with the showing of interest will the outcome of this generosity be gratitude.

In business, perhaps it is high wages or low wages that affect the workers' attitude to their employers. I doubt this to be true, believing that it is fairness in wages that affects how employees regard their employers. If the employees feel that they are treated fairly, they will work happily. If not, then they will never be content, regardless of how high their wages are. They will always feel that they are being cheated and will consequently resent their employers' success. The leaders who concentrate on behaving with fairness are the ones who will have love from their employees, success in their efforts and, of the most importance to those who direct industry, lasting fame.

20

How Flatterers are Avoided.

FLATTERY AND FALSE PROFITS

I do not want to leave aside an important matter, a mistake that it is easy for a Prince to make unless he is very prudent and has good judgement. This concerns flatterers, of which the courts are full, for men become so obsessed with their own affairs, deceiving themselves in the process, that it is difficult to defend themselves from this plague. In seeking to combat it, one runs the risk of becoming hated. There is no other defence against flattery than letting men know that they do not offend you by telling you the truth. But when everybody feels able to tell you the truth, you lose respect.

What Machiavelli does not say, however, is that when people tell you the truth, that truth is not necessarily the truth, only the truth as they perceive it. He continues to suggest that you need people to tell you the truth, but only in regard to subjects on which they are expert. This, I am afraid, asks too much of human nature, for the habit of mankind is to give you views on subjects about which you know rather more than they. Their words can be seen as a form of torture invented for their pleasure and your pain. Only a patient person could possibly put up with these people telling their truths. This, I suppose, is why the flatterers of the world find such a ready audience among both great princes and great employers.

Machiavelli's advice to avoid flatterers has never appealed to me. I am of the view that those who advise need to give sympathy and understanding to princes. Their words, however, are often dismissed as flattery by those who desire to replace them in the affections and counsel of leaders. I also believe that those who command with certainty and success will pay no heed to soothing words. The words of flatterers can only help leaders deal with the stresses and strains of their position. The flatterer is a necessary element in the court of any political party or business. A flatterer will never succeed in misleading a true leader.

Machiavelli's suggestion that flatterers are only permitted to give advice when it is asked for is a system employed by most of the European royal families. "A Prince therefore ought always to take counsel, but only when he wishes and not when others wish. He ought rather to discourage everyone from offering advice unless he asks it." This is a system that has not had much success, as the fate of the royal families in Europe testifies. A leader of people does not need advice and so when a flatterer gives seductive advice, or advises in the flatterer's own interest, the true leader will hear the words and smile, for it is amusing to be so flattered.

In business, the words of flatterers do not matter—in business only results count. Measurable results soon uncover flatterers who pretend to be advisers. In politics, it is only the wisdom of the political leader that can spot flatterers for what they are. The future of that leader may well depend on how flatterers and their words are treated. The leader must allow practiced flatterers to flatter but never promote nor reject them. Here, however, we deal with business and there we find flattery in by far its most dangerous form. A form of flattery that is not uncommon in business is called "massaging the accounts."

Chairpersons and directors are often flattered by a success that does not in reality exist. The accounts are written in such a way that there appear to be large profits. Those who write about business praise the efforts of that corporation's directors, flattering them without realizing that they have become a part of this conceit. The value of the corporation's shares rises and its board meetings become jolly affairs. The directors boast and quote the success of their company; the banks are eager to lend money to this corporation and listen with rapt attention to the words of its chairperson; the chairperson is invited to sit on other boards, and confidently passes on the secret of an apparent success. All is false, all is flattery. The high price of this corporation's shares make a cheap and therefore easy way for it to take over other corporations, changing their inflated shares for the good shares of that corporation's victims. The latter may have cash in the bank, but appear pedestrian and lackluster beside the spectacular triumph of the now-great corporation. One day, for any of a number of little reasons, events move against this great corporation and it is seen for what it is—an empty bladder. Now its board meetings become savage affairs; the shareholders scream with anger as they lose the possibility of profits from their shares; banks who have happily taken millions in interest payments require a return of their capital with a haste that is tantamount to defrauding the shareholders of their money. Worst of all, the corporation's employees who gained nothing and worked with the intention of risking nothing, lose their jobs. They lose their jobs without warning or compensation, or even sympathy. Often these industrial tragedies happen at a time when work is short and not readily available. Such is the real danger of flattery, when it is believed.

The fanciful words of an individual who dabbles in flattery are as nothing to the damage caused by the collective conceit of a corporation's management when it engages in the pursuit of illusionary success. Things become even worse when they use this illusion of success to pursue personal prestige and preferment. Deceiving others, while undesirable is often, in its complexity, capable of being admired, but to deceive oneself is always detestable. Do not, however, dismiss flattery out of hand, for there will be many occasions when you need to use that dubious art. Always remember that flattery is the infantry of negotiations.

21

Whether Fortresses and Many Other Things Commonly Used by Princes are Useful or Useless.

STRUCTURING THE BUSINESS

Some Princes, in order to hold on to their states securely, have disarmed their subjects, some have kept their subject towns divided, and some have fostered animosity against themselves.

Here Machiavelli outlines two structural systems, which employers may institute to maintain internal control of their businesses. The first removes the power of decision making from their line management and branch offices, keeping this power among a small clique at head office, or just to themselves. The second plays one branch office against another, creating what is called by some "creative tension," and by others, an unnecessary impediment to the business of getting on with their work. Machiavelli offers a third: "Others have fostered enmities against themselves." This is, of course, another form of "creative tension," which some employers believe keeps their employees alert. These employers keep their senior staff in a state of perpetual fear, digging at them with words, driving them with threats, always leaving them wondering if they will still have employment the next day. A fourth system is used by those who "have laid themselves out to gain over those whom they distrusted in the beginning of their governments." Ensconced in a new company, this type of chairperson tries to seduce their senior staff with flamboyant kindness and cloying attention to detail of their employees' personal lives, effecting a style of overbearing goodness, hoping that soon they will be loved and therefore secure. Others still "have built fortresses"—established management systems that appear foolproof. Of course, here it is worth remembering that systems which work wonderfully with ordinary people are completely useless with fools. A fool will act irrationally and in folly, and it is almost impossible for anyone of intelligence to predict just how a fool will behave. Some who chair companies prefer not to have complicated systems and to work in a more hands-on fashion, others just enjoy changing whatever exists when they arrive. This is a habit born of caution and a desire to dominate, that as it grows old becomes a total conceit. "And although one cannot give a final judgement on all these things unless one possesses the particulars of those states [businesses] in which a decision has to be made, nevertheless I will speak as comprehensively as the matter itself will admit."

Machiavelli believed that it was better to spread power than to centralize it. He is right, of course, for then the energy, brains and enthusiasm of many are at your disposal. The direction of the company may, however, be weakened in this way. To avoid this it is better to consult with many, but to decide for yourself. Give the impression that you are interested in the ideas of others, but never bind yourself to agree with those ideas and to carry them out. Policy decisions must be your own and, in this respect, the company must be run from one base.

Solutions are seldom composed of a single thought, more often they are made up of an amalgam of thoughts. Explain this when asking for advice and bitterness will be avoided later. "By arming them, those arms become yours. Those men who were distrusted become faithful, and those who were faithful are kept so and your subjects [employees] become your adherents." It is, of course, completely impractical to ask everyone's advice; such a habit can only lead to the most terrible confusion and resultant ill-will. "Whereas all subjects cannot be armed [given responsibility], yet when those whom you do arm are benefited, the others can be handled more freely and this difference in their treatment, which they quite understand, makes the former your dependents, and the latter, considering it to be necessary that those who have the most danger and service, should have the most reward, excuse you."

Most people do not want responsibility, only job security. Therefore, if responsibility is given to others, most people do not feel aggrieved. If, however, no responsibility is given to anyone, then most people will imagine that they want this previously unsought responsibility. Soon, anger will begin to seethe among all the employees. Do not forget that if employees are commanded by those who work at the same place as they do and if they are commanded by those who are known to them, then they will feel that their colleagues who have this responsibility will be more aware of their needs. "But when you disarm them [take away responsibility] you at once offend them by showing that you distrust them either for cowardice or lack of loyalty."

Never, never demote anyone. Get rid of them if they will not work with others or promote them away from those others if you believe that they have indispensable talent. Never make one person subservient to another when that person has previously had independence or worked in a senior position, for such a move will only end in failure. Under these circumstances, anyone of talent will leave and the work of those who stay becomes lackadaisical.

When you have to dismiss an employee, always do this in such a way that the dismissed employees feel that they have been promoted. Find them a better job, or merely tell them that they are far too good for your organization and a fine future lies ahead of them working elsewhere. Remember, there is always a sense of relief that follows the initial shock of dismissal. Take advantage of this phenomenon and give the bad news one day and then praise them the next. Always be lavish in a person's going and do not spare expense on leaving parties and the like.

When you have developed a power structure in your business that seems to work, do not disrupt that structure by the use of consultants or temporary staff. As we have seen, Machiavelli does not think well of mercenaries: "Even if they should be good they would not be sufficient to defend you against powerful enemies and distrusted subjects." In general, temporary staff will be idle, at best having no reason to work hard, and at worst, mischievous. Consultants will charge too much and the results will be small and in all likelihood the recommendations of consultants will mostly benefit those consultants.

As for ruling by dividing your staff, Machiavelli dismisses this principle. "I do not believe that factions can ever be of use; rather it is certain that when the enemy comes upon you in divided cities you are quickly lost, because the weakest party will always assist the outside forces and the others will not be able to resist." To divide and rule is the resort of the truly insecure. It is an instinct rather than a craft, an instinct that invariably becomes conceit. As a method of management it is not at all efficient and carries with it many risks.

"Without doubt, Princes become great when they over-come the difficulties and obstacles by which they are con-fronted, and therefore Fortune, when she desires to make a new Prince great who has a greater necessity to earn renown than a hereditary one, causes enemies to arise and form designs against him in order that he may have the op-portunity of overcoming them and by them to mount higher, as by a ladder which his enemies have raised."

It is true that when a new chairperson or managing di-rector takes over a company it is common for that person to stamp their own style on the venture. Machiavelli suggests that luck may give them the opportunity to do that. What is more, he goes on to suggest that really cunning people may very well invent problems that they know they can resolve. "For this reason, many consider that a wise Prince, when he has the opportunity, ought with craft to foster animosity against himself, so that having crushed it, his renown may rise higher." This passage in *The Prince* comes as no surprise, for what Machiavelli recommends is an Italian instinct and you can barely go a day in modern Italy without coming across numerous examples of this wretched practice. It is not a very satisfactory strategy as far as an employer is con-cerned. There is no more irritating a habit in an employee than that of inventing imaginary problems which, with great pride, he or she can resolve. For a chairperson to practice such an activity shows only the need for continual reassur-ance and that such a person is not fit to rule. This principle of creating false problems also has the serious weakness that it is totally transparent and not worthy of either Machiavelli or his students. There may, however, be just one possible use for this device, and that is to create a false problem which is easily seen to be false, so that while all watch you triumph over a problem that does not exist, you are up to other nefarious deeds behind their backs. As a distraction, the false problem is excellent; as a device for establishing credentials it is a disaster.

"Princes, especially new ones, have found more fidelity and assistance in those men who in the beginnings of their Rule were distrusted than amongst those who were trusted." This seems a perverse precept, and Machiavelli covers his back by writing: "On this question one cannot speak generally, for it varies too much with the individual." Machiavelli goes on to suggest that these rebels make excellent staff: "They know it to be very necessary for them to cancel by deeds the bad impression which he had formed of them; and thus the Prince always extracts more profit from them than from those who serving him in too much security, may neglect his affairs." The person who moves to a position of power should hesitate before introducing a clean decks policy, for troublemakers and rebels are people of character. If their energy is turned to the right uses, then they usually excel. Strangely, troublemakers and rebels are seldom leaders, for, being natural critics, they fear the responsibility of decision. They are just people cast in the wrong mold and only when allied to a leader will they be successful. However, they are always uncomfortable for a leader to have around, for, being people of principle, even if those principles are misconceived, their sensibilities are easily offended. Having changed sides once, they may do so again and become intractable enemies. Machiavelli writes, "We shall find that it is easier for the Prince to make friends of those men who were contented under the former Government and are therefore his enemies, than those who being discontented with it, were favourable to him and encouraged him to seize it." These former enemies of the prince have shown that they are not cheaply bought or easily offended by the prince straying from the purity of their beliefs.

"It has been a custom with Princes, in order to hold their states more securely, to build fortresses that may serve as a bridle and bit to those who design to work against them." Some who run companies create systems that remove authority from those who manage, prescribing exactly how they should perform. At first glance, such a system seems to work and in truth often does work in the beginning. As the business grows, so does the system and those charged with supervising it; but in turn, managers become remote from those they manage and the business becomes vulnerable. "Fortresses therefore are useful or not, according to circumstances; if they do you good in one way, they injure you in another and this question can be reasoned thus: the Prince who has more to fear from the people than from foreigners ought to build fortresses, but he who has more to fear from foreigners than from his people ought to leave them alone."

The best system for the best managers is a simple system. Machiavelli writes, "All these things considered then, I shall praise him who builds fortresses [holds power in the head office and institutes complicated systems] as well as him who does not [leaves power in branch offices and has simple systems]. And I shall blame whoever, trusting in them [having systems or not having systems] cares little about being hated by the people."

As Machiavelli points out, in the end, it does not greatly matter which system is best. The safety of a business and the one who runs that business really lies in the quality of the product and the ability of those who manage the making of that product. The balance of systems in a business and where those systems are located, whether in the head office, or the branch offices, depends on the style of the one who runs that business. Those who have courage and fear in the right proportions need not have the false reassurance of complicated systems. Furthermore, the safety of all lies in how they are led, combined with the brilliance of the strategy conceived by the one who decides where they are led.

22

On the Things for which Men, and especially Princes, are Praised or Blamed.

THE COMPANY IMAGE

But since my intention is to write something useful for the understanding reader, it seems to me more beneficial to go behind to the effectual truth of the matter, rather than focusing on the imagining of it.

Machiavelli clearly understood the differences between the perceived truth and the actual truth and I have no doubt that he, in all probability, understood that the perceived truth, once it has become generally accepted, changes its nature to become the actual truth as far as mankind is concerned.

The world, and the humans who inhabit it, do not like to appear foolish, and this is exactly what would happen should they be convinced to accept the real truth, having already accepted the perceived truth. Those who offer the real, but often unpalatable, truth, when all people believe in another truth of their own invention, fall into the category of the messenger who brings bad news. Never engage in this activity, for it is a total waste of time and highly dangerous. The views of mankind are changed only a little at a time and these changes must be composed of conclusions that they have arrived at themselves.

A ripple of goodwill is the way to successfully promote a person or a business. The frontal attack, while often apparently successful, creates its own danger: the hurdle of success. Success creates jealousy and jealousy is the breeding ground of treachery. Sudden success is the most fertile of all ground for jealousy to thrive in. The ripple of gossip is created by the judicious use of men and women who are either natural or hired gossips. Natural gossips are marginally better in the respect that they work for the price of a lunch or two, and for the pleasure of gossiping. They also work in a more discreet fashion, spreading the fame of your business and yourself. Their words create an atmosphere of goodwill and they are believed because they have no apparent motive, and, in time, the ripple becomes a wave.

The hired gossip goes about this work with more method and the result is much the same, but achieved with greater speed. However, there is the risk that in using such people you expose your hand. All people in the business of promotion, knowing well their trade, will understand what is being attempted and perhaps it may be in the interest of some of them to frustrate your efforts. This ripple of goodwill can then become a ripple of ill will, if used by other people against you, and as discussed earlier, it is far better in all your dealings, as far as is possible never to leave enemies behind you.

It is important never, under any circumstances, to believe your own publicity. The one who would use the advantages of the perceived truth must know clearly that what is being used, and that the wonderful things which are said or written, are only the perceived truth, the fantasies invented for a purpose. Never, never, convince yourself that the perceived truth has become the real truth, even though that perceived truth may very well have become the accepted truth. There is no honor in self-deception.

Avoid personal publicity unless that publicity is necessary to promote your business. Personal publicity brings with it jealousy in quarters where you least expect jealousy to be found. This jealousy festers, for at first it is a silent jealousy, but it may not remain silent for long. Always ask of yourself what is to be gained from this publicity before agreeing to it. If the answer to your question is nothing, do not touch the wretched thing and keep a distance from those who engage in publicity and places where publicity abounds.

Never use the media by selling them a notion which is untrue, for they will resent this deception. Never use others to promote a particular notion without telling them that this is what they do, for they will resent being used. Let your myth and the myth of your company be built on the ripple of goodwill. Let your reputation become one of achieving that which you say you will achieve, rather than one for saying that you will achieve great things and never fulfilling these promises. Remember always that mystery is far more intriguing than the words of one who perpetually boasts. Let those who deal in publicity come to their own conclusions. There is no need to tell them everything about your affairs.

In the same way, if you wish to destroy an opponent by a building ripple of criticism, the technique must have subtlety. For instance, suggest that your opponent is a fine person who has done much good work. Praise that opponent and then add, "I greatly admire (whatever that one's name may be) however, you must remember always that he is a . . . (and state his nationality)." There is nothing in general about nationals from any country that is either dubious or second-rate. However, the juxtaposition of the compliment and the caveat that the person is of a particular nationality turns the compliment into a warning that is so unspecific it is impossible to put your finger on just what is wrong with the person. If the one who compliments that person so lavishly implies that they have doubts, then the people to whom this person is unknown must feel, if they are prudent, extremely uncertain about that person's reliability. The attack delivered with the greatest subtlety is the hardest attack to combat and soon that ripple of criticism has reached the proportions of a tidal wave.

Always remember that while extreme success will create jealousy and envy, the results of that envy and jealousy will not become apparent until you strike hard times. Prepare always for such hard times by leaving friends behind you, and if you must have enemies, let them always be in front of you.

Machiavelli continues, "For many have pictured republics and principalities which in fact have never been known or seen, because how one lives is so distant from how one ought to live, that he who neglects what is done for what ought to be done sooner effects his ruin than his preservation; for a man who wishes to act entirely up to his professions of virtue soon meets with what destroys him among so much that is evil."

Never overpromote either people or ideas, for then failure in both is inevitable and the cost of that failure is great. Machiavelli writes, "Hence, it is necessary for a Prince wishing to hold his own to know how to do wrong and to make use of it or not, according to necessity." To do wrong does not always bring acrimony. In fact, so perverse is life, that far more acrimony is likely to come your way from doing right rather than wrong.

Here is a story that illustrates how a bad deed can be made to appear as a good deed. A woman is run down by a wealthy man in a smart car and, as she sits on the curb with her damaged bicycle beside her, she feels nothing but anger at her situation and the wrong that has been done to her. She has, without doubt, been the victim of a bad deed. The man takes her into a nearby hotel and buys her several large dry martinis. In time, they emerge and the man picks up the woman's bicycle, spins its wheels and sends the woman on her way. The bad deed is forgotten: now all this woman thinks of is the smartness of the hotel and the dry martinis, the like of which she had never come across before. By virtue of how the man handled this situation, the bad deed has become a good deed. Arriving home, the woman tells her son that she met such a nice man who bought her a few dry martinis in a smart hotel. This woman is filled with goodwill towards the stranger, forgetting that there would have been no need for the man's kindness if he had not wrongfully harmed her by knocking her down in the first place.

Machiavelli continues, "Therefore, putting on one side imaginary things concerning a Prince and discussing those which are real, I say that all men when they are spoken of, and chiefly Princes, for being more highly placed, are remarkable for some of the qualities which bring them either blame or praise, and then it is that one is reputed liberal, another miserly, using a Tuscan term (because an avaricious person in our language is still he who desires to possess by robbery, whilst we call one miserly who deprives himself too much of the use of his own) one is reputed generous, one rapacious, one cruel, one compassionate, one faithless another faithful, one effeminate and cowardly, another bold and brave. One affable, another haughty; one lascivious, another chaste; one sincere, another cunning; one hard, another easy; one grave, another frivolous; one religious, another unbelieving; and the like."

Those who run a business must be all of these things, for all of these characteristics must be in the armory of employers, and they must know when and where to use each of them. Although it is necessary to use all these characteristics, it is equally necessary to appear only to use those that people believe to be good characteristics. Hence, it is necessary to have the wave of goodwill to cover the moments when the bad characteristics must be used. That may seem improbable, for why would a person need to be cowardly? It is simply that there will be times when cowardice is wisdom, and bravery folly. The person who will succeed must judge well the occasion to use each of these. Never forget, as Machiavelli points out, "that it would be most praiseworthy in a Prince to exhibit all the above qualities that are considered good; but because they can neither be entirely possessed nor observed, for human conditions do not permit it, it is necessary for him to be sufficiently prudent that he may know how to avoid the reproach of those vices which would lose him his state." You need not only a skill in making judgments, but also an ability to present those judgments in a light that will reflect well on you and your business.

Here I would like to draw on the words of Mark Twain, a sage who was quite as well versed in cunning as Machiavelli, for advice when dealing with those who write in the press or who own newspapers. Mark Twain was of the view that you should never pick a quarrel with a man who buys his printer's ink by the barrel. Always maintain a good relationship with journalists, editors and proprietors. Never lobby the latter against the former and never complain and cause a journalist to suffer a reprimand or the sack, for that journalist will turn up again working for someone else, still writing, with an even larger grudge against you.

When questioned by the press, the maintenance of silence is often an efficient tactic. Without a quote, even if that quote is only made of the words, "No comment," a journalist may find it hard to write a story. If, however, the journalist is in the possession of numerous facts, the journalist already has a story and a refusal to answer questions will be construed as an admission of guilt. Then is the time to speak, finding out from the journalist all that he or she knows while telling the journalist a tale that is so vacuous in its content and boring in the telling, that no editor would print it. If you do wish to be quoted, use words that are sharp, witty or cleverly put together. However, if you wish to avoid being quoted speak in ill-put-together sentences at great length and in a slow, methodical manner. If you wish to divine how much the journalist knows, then delay answering, for in a silence people will say words that they later regret.

A journalist who tries to discover how much you know will put a statement to you that is both provocative and inaccurate, because even the cleverest of people can rarely resist correcting an inaccurate statement. In such a way will you be drawn into a discussion that can only be to your disadvantage. Make it quite clear on what terms you will tell anything to a journalist and never tell a journalist anything that you would regret reading in print. If you would preempt a story by telling it in confidence, be sure that your judgment is right in whom you expect to honor that confidence. Finally, when dealing with the press, always remember that you try to persuade them to print the version of a story that suits your purpose. Others do the same, so do not take what you read in the newspapers as suitable evidence for making decisions.

In the cause of promoting the reputation of your business, you will have to appear in public and, because the perception of the message that you wish to convey is all important to the success of your business, your image is all important. For people, when they hear other people speak, do not carefully listen to their words. The information that they draw from a person's appearance is, in many ways, as important as the words that person utters. Messages are received by both the ears and the eyes and then relayed to the memory. The words used to convey a message will be colored by people's overall impressions. Therefore image is of vital importance, for image is a shorthand. It is a way of telling others of the accumulated wisdom of many years, a way of them instantly becoming aware of the character and style of the author. A particular tie, a particular mode of dress, style of hair, type of shoe, all have preconceived associations for those who watch. An accent indicates, often wrongly, a level of education; cigars, a level of wealth; a certain car, a level of success. The conclusions reached by others, using your image as evidence, are most likely to be wrong—this, however, does not matter. What matters is that your image, true or false, has led others to those conclusions. You must take all this into account when you deal with them.

In this public side to your life, you may well find that you have to make speeches. Many books have been written on the art of public speaking. However, I doubt if any of them has recommended the use of a false impediment of speech. A sudden stutter in a speech draws the attention of the audience. They believe that you may break down and so wait, alert, for that moment. When speaking, never tread on laughter that you cause by starting a new sentence until that laughter is finished. An audience does not understand what you say until several moments after you have said the words. Never stop applause unless you wish to make a dramatic effect and only at the end of the speech. Then finish and walk away. The result is stunning. Use short sentences and use repetition often, repeating a particular idea using slightly different words, time and time again. A sentence left hanging out of place in a speech is very effective as it makes the audience think. Remember that all public speaking is about rhythm. Do not speak unless you are able to speak with ability. If you do not have natural ability, take lessons in public speaking. It is a great mistake to expose yourself to failure—the one who would succeed should avoid all exposure to unnecessary danger, for such exposure is not courage, merely conceit.

23

On the Avoidance of Contempt and Hatred.

PUBLIC RELATIONS

The Prince, as hinted at above, should seek to avoid those things that render him odious and contemptible. Whenever he avoids them, he will have fulfilled his job and will find that his other evil actions pose no threat to him at all.

In success, the criticism of others is of little account, only the self-knowledge of how you attained that success is important. Has your success been attained with honor, or did you come by this apparent success dishonorably? If the latter is true, then however great your success may seem to others, there will surely come a moment when you will see your success as shoddy and tainted. Do not, however, for one moment believe that honorable success will be rewarded with the admiration of others, for the reverse is true. Success will only bring you apparent admiration and the jealousy of others. Certainly those who hope to benefit from your success will speak admiringly of you, and those close to you may genuinely admire your achievements. However, human nature likes nothing better than to destroy the successful person.

The one who engages in business has various options. The businessperson may choose to live privately and in an upright manner, putting aside all manner of excess, seeking no publicity and never promoting himself. Such a person lives in the hope that their efforts to improve the wealth of themselves and their family will pass unnoticed. Those involved in finance, which at its best is an anonymous business, can often conduct their affairs in such a way, but a person whose business is his own creation and which is involved with that person's identity, cannot do this.

Another option is for the businessperson to learn the art of dealing with the media, using all the tricks that go with that trade—such as the false defeat: when a person seems to lose, in order to gain public sympathy, or the false triumph: where a person seems to win in order to appear strong—thus giving credibility to any number of dubious propositions that person may wish to make in the future. Neither of these ploys are examples of the use of true facts, rather of false facts given to the media to chew on, much as a dog chews on a bone. Another useful ploy is the false accusation. First, create a situation where you are wrongly accused. Then, at a convenient moment, arrange for the false accusation to be shown to be false beyond all doubt. Those who have made accusations against both the company and its management become discredited. Further accusations will then be treated with great suspicion. Always remember that people's memories are very frail, remembering only both the high spots and the lows of a person's career, and then seldom remembering accurately. People believe in the facts that it suits them to believe.

People find it easy to believe the facts that are offered to them, if they want to believe them, and easy to disbelieve those facts, if they do not want to believe them. Even in the highest levels of business, these apparent facts are seldom checked or investigated in any depth. The information that circulates in business is generally gleaned from the newspapers and specialist agencies who print newsletters. However, most of the important information that circulates is the product of gossip. To counterbalance this, there are those in the business world who use this to their own advantage by spreading different rumors to defeat ones already in circulation. They call this promoting the truth. The truth that we know, however, is the truth that it suits each of us to know.

Thus, when employing a person to handle your public relations, it is wise to observe a number of rules. First, as I have written before, never tell these people more than they need to know. There is no more indiscreet type of person than those who deal in the twitching of images. They deal in the spreading of gossip dressed up as fact. Tell such a person anything and you must expect them to pass what you tell on to others. You must use these men and women, but never let them use you and your reputation.

Reputation is what other people believe, so never neglect to inform them of your successes and keep secret from them your failures. Particularly take trouble to impress the people whom you have hired to promote you with your abilities and successes. They will believe these things because they are paid for their work and they will be more successful in promoting you. Always follow your own intuition about the actions you must take. Never take the advice of these image twitchers except on how to present the actions, once taken. Image twitchers have a specific talent for doing a specific job. Nevertheless, they are salespeople and they will try to sell you many things, about most of which they know little, including the idea that they are both tacticians and great strategists. Do not buy miscellaneous goods from such people.

Machiavelli warns against hatred, which is a totally different emotion from the normal jealousy of people and has about it a capricious quality. Hatred is a hard and enduring emotion. When you are hated, there is little that you can do about the matter, for hatred is irrational and burns the soul of the one who hates and infects the life of the object of that hatred. "It makes him hated above all things, as I have said, to be rapacious, and to be a violator of the property and women of his subjects [customers and employees], from both of which he must abstain." It should not be hard to follow most of this advice.

However, surprisingly, a great number of employers ravage the pension funds of their employees. At first, they merely sell a property that is surplus to their requirements to the pension fund that belongs to their staff. This is dressed up with independent valuations conducted by valuers whose independence is in doubt because of their hope to receive future business from the company. In good times, such employers scrape off the surplus cash from the company's pension schemes, for the schemes are overfunded, not by the brilliance of investment but by the fact that times are good. When times are hard, these people reject pretense altogether, taking money from the pension funds without even the pretense of a legal justification. Machiavelli continues, "And when neither property nor honour is touched, the majority of men lie content." Here Machiavelli touches on a point far more likely to cause trouble for an employer than tinkering with a pension fund. An employee's most valuable possession is honor; never damage the ego of those who work for you and always be meticulous in avoiding situations where employees may be humiliated.

Contempt is easily acquired by dithering and overreacting in a crisis or even turning an everyday event into a crisis. Machiavelli writes, "It makes him contemptible to be considered fickle, frivolous, effeminate, mean-spirited, irresolute, from all of which a Prince should guard himself." Here help from a twitcher of images is invaluable. Machiavelli continues, "He should endeavour to show in his actions greatness, courage, gravity and fortitude." These two passages are the perfect brief for a twitcher of images. It is that person's job to present the client in this way to the public. Privately, Machiavelli continues, all is different: "And in his private dealings with his subjects, let him show that his judgements are irrevocable." To the public the great employer must appear sweet reason itself, while to employees there must be that hint of fear.

Machiavelli seems to write in favor of the twitchers of images: "That Prince is highly esteemed who conveys this impression of himself and he who is highly esteemed is not easily conspired against." And further: "He who is well armed will have good friends and affairs will always remain quiet when they are quiet without, unless they should have been already disturbed by conspiracy." By using half-truths and convenient words, the image twitcher's job is to make certain that the world knows that the employer is well armed. In effect, "strength makes strength" is as true as its correlation that "weakness brings weakness." The one who fails is truly in danger, for that one is a natural victim for others who wish to succeed. In Machiavelli's words, one must "maintain himself in such reputation that no one can hope to deceive him or get round him." This is self-delusion on a grand scale. Great employers must always believe that people will try to deceive them, for these people seek their own ends and there is always a strong possibility that if they are not recognized for what they are, they will succeed. The great employer must always suspect the natures of those who come with simple propositions.

Can the twitcher of images sniff out treachery and self-interest? It is doubtful for that is not the trade of image twitchers. In time, despite the twitcher's best endeavors, the reality of any situation will overtake the image twitcher's efforts and he will leave the amiable employer in the lurch. It would be in the image twitcher's self-interest to do so, for even those who twitch images cannot afford to work for a failure. After all, even he needs to earn a living, and no one is as attuned to changes in the wind as he.

Machiavelli deals at some length with the effect that outside opinion has on the behavior of employees, and vice versa. "And one of the most efficacious remedies that a Prince can have against conspiracies is not to be hated and despised by the people, for he who conspires against a Prince always expects to please them by his [the Prince's] removal; but when the conspirator can only look forward to offending, then he will not have the courage to take such a course, for the difficulties that confront a conspirator are infinite." A good public image may be based on conceit, but that is not its true importance. The good public image will influence shareholders in your business and more importantly institutional investors, who are much impressed by the views of the public. Furthermore, it is equally important to preserve a good image with your customers, not only so that they continue to buy your goods, but also because in times of danger, rebellion and internal treachery, they will side with you. Twitchers of images can be helpful in all these matters: always remember that if the image of a business is propitious, there is little to fear from conspiracy.

It is the task of the image twitcher to keep in place all the benefits that Machiavelli describes, but it is equally the task of the employer to seek out and destroy the treacherous yet obliging employee. "On the side of the conspirator there is nothing but fear and jealousy and the prospect of punishment to terrify him; but on the side of the Prince there is the majesty of the principality, the laws, the protection of friends and the state to defend him: so that adding to all these things the popular goodwill, it is impossible that any should be rash enough to conspire." These are Machiavelli's words on the subject of conspirators, but he later notes, "that such like deaths which are deliberately inflicted with a resolved and desperate courage cannot be avoided by Princes, because anyone who does not fear to die can inflict them." In fact, beware the madman with nothing to lose and, indeed, beware the person who wishes to lose everything (though, in Machiavelli's words, "A Prince may fear them the less because they are very rare"). The one who would rise to be great in business cannot afford to take such a casual attitude to such people. They must be noticed as their personalities change, their habits change, their appearance changes, indeed their size and shape changes. These people whom we call mad are not born this way, they change during their lives. Their madness or determination becoming uppermost in their characters, takes the form of purity of thought and any infringement on that purity has to be punished whatever the cost to themselves.

Always remember the circumstances for treachery are never impossible, for the conceit of mankind will make no folly too grand for the overcoming of both caution and cowardice. The image twitcher is an invaluable assistant in battles from within and can also help create an atmosphere that makes battle less likely. The image twitcher, however, cannot guarantee safety. It is better to be loved than hated, but this love must only be a shroud that hides fear, and it is the job of the twitcher of images to stitch the many strands of the fabric of this shroud together. Remember, however, that the fabrics of the shroud are only apparent respect, apparent love, apparent loyalty all created by apparent success, rather than reality. When failure comes, all such emotion will disappear and the employer must strive hard to maintain self-respect, let alone the respect of others. In this situation, the twitcher of images is of little help. The employer who would be great cannot depend entirely on the help of others or indeed the love and loyalty of others. This employer must arm himself with the sheathed sword of fear and a skeptical attitude towards both people and situations.

The employer's most important question must be "Why?" and it must be asked frequently.

In whatever dire straits a person engaging in business may find themselves, such a person must always strive to retain their self-respect, for that self-respect will be their salvation during hard times. You should take care not to part with your self-respect cheaply on your rise in business, for the time will come when your self-respect is of incredible value and without self-respect you will be entirely lost.

24

How a Prince Should Act in Order to Gain Reputation.

THE ADVANTAGES AND DANGERS OF FAME

Nothing makes a Prince more highly esteemed than the assumption of great undertakings and striking examples of his own ability.

Machiavelli refers to the building of fine palaces when he writes of great enterprises; such a way is the politician's road to fame. The best modern example of such a practice was the rule of President Mitterrand in France, where there is barely a monument that this President did not paint gold or a town in that country which does not have some vast new building as a testament to President Mitterrand's apparent power and glory. The reality of France's situation during the rule of that President is a rather different matter.

For individuals engaging in business, the only enterprises that must be glorious are the companies in their charge. Nothing must ever be allowed to distract from this aim, all else is conceit. Only consider a chase after publicity if you are sure that such publicity will help your company to do better business. Only involve yourself in publicity for which there is a positive purpose, for all publicity carries the danger of being disadvantageous. Do not incur unnecessary risks, for business is already too full of necessary ones. Publicity must never be sought just for the sake of publicity. Such publicity is purely to promote the person not the business. However, sometimes it appears that the person and the business are one and the same, and this can prove dangerous, for in these circumstances the person is tempted to believe that all publicity undertaken is good publicity. This temptation must be resisted and always remember that publicity is a drug as insidious and dangerous as all drugs. There can come a time when the victims of this drug long to see their names in the newspapers and their faces on television even if the comment that goes with such publicity is harmful. Such people will take actions and decisions to gain publicity rather than to further the success of their business.

Charitable giving is about advancement in social status and has little or nothing to do with business, or for that matter charity. The giving of large sums of money to charities in the most public of fashions is a promotion of self and an extravagant form of promoting your business. Many would argue that to give money to charity advances your social status, and hence your ability to capture the best business deals; such arguments are self-serving. In any case, the most famous people these days are the greatest criminals, not the greatest saints. A reputation for modesty, honor and integrity, while generally considered a better way to fame, is not the fastest way to fame. Furthermore, such a reputation will make you the target of every cheapskate and swindler that comes across your name. Far better to have a reputation for a general toughness in business, a reputation for taking terrible revenge on those that cheat you. Such a reputation is of far more use than a reputation for mindless generosity.

Machiavelli uses the career of Ferdinand of Aragon as an example of how a prince can use his reputation to advance his position. Ferdinand of Aragon was but an insignificant prince until he started on his rise to fame. "He did this quietly at first, and without any fear of hindrance, for he held the minds of the Barons of Castile occupied in thinking of war and not anticipating any innovations." Ferdinand of Aragon must have, as have a number of modern-day tycoons, convinced the public and his competitors that he was of little consequence. In so doing, he caused them to underestimate his ability, his resolve and his cunning.

When engaging in publicity, consider very carefully the form that publicity takes, for the person who publicizes his or her brilliance is immediately at a disadvantage, while the clever person who publicizes only follies has a hidden strength. However, bear in mind that the one who publicizes extravagance alerts those who would lend money, so that person must also publicize financial success. "Then they did not perceive that by these means he was acquiring power and authority over them. He was able, with the money of the church and of the people, to sustain his armies and by that long war to lay the foundation for military skill which has since distinguished him. Further, using religion as a plea, so as to undertake greater schemes, he devoted himself with a pious cruelty to driving out and cleaning his kingdom of the Moors." This is a fine example of a man who used publicity to his own advantage. He publicized his piety in order to gain support from the church, then borrowed the church's money and used that money for his own ends, thus clearing his country of enemies. Remember that publicity does not need to be true. However, to be effective, the people need to be able to believe that publicity is true. It is easier to construct a thought that people already believe, or wish to believe, and to promote that thought, changing it subtly, than it is to try and change old beliefs or new longings.

Having gained power through support won by apparent piety, Ferdinand of Aragon used this position and "under this same cloak, he assailed Africa, he came down on Italy, he has finally attacked France." This man never publicized his intention, never boasted of great schemes that were in his mind, "and his actions have arisen in such a way, one out of the other that men have never been given time to work steadily against him." The danger with raising the image of a person in business is that their high profile makes them newsworthy and so they attract publicity. Astute competitors are then able to predict their moves while their publicity only impresses those of no consequence.

Publicity and the image of princes should be formed these days by small events, acts of individual kindness or consideration, not vast gestures invented solely to impress the masses: the invitation to a party, for instance, sent to a person long retired and, although formerly of much use to you, now of little consequence as far as your affairs are concerned. Remembering people from the past always impresses those for whom "the past" is fast approaching. Machiavelli is surprisingly enthusiastic about giving parties. "Further, he [the Prince or employer] ought to entertain the people [employees or customers]. With festivals and spectacles at convenient seasons of the year, as every city [company] is divided into guilds or into societies, he ought to hold such bodies [the various clubs and trade organizations] in esteem, and associate with them sometimes, and show himself an example of courtesy and liberality. Always maintaining the majesty of his rank. For this, he must never consent to abate in anything."

When giving parties, always remember to surround clients with important people. People who believe themselves to be important like to be surrounded by other important people. People who are unimportant to the world, but of vital importance to your undertakings, will be flattered and imagine themselves to be as important as those with whom they rub shoulders. Always mix important people in with unimportant people, for important people, once they have established in their own minds that these parties are for important people, will wish to seek out an audience to listen to their wisdom.

Always remember that the effect of a party is not how much people enjoy themselves while they are there, rather the pleasure that the people get from talking to their friends about the other guests who were at the party with them. Never split your parties into two, with some guests invited to dine and less important guests only invited to drink. Such a habit will only lead to anger, particularly on the part of those who know that they are less important but do not want that fact demonstrated publicly. When placing people at your table, always put together those who can be useful to each other in business — they will be suitably grateful if they profit from your parties. Food and drink is of the utmost importance and a reputation for the very best wine and the cooking of fine food will ensure that the most important people attend your parties. Talleyrand, the great European diplomat of the nineteenth century, used this principle — his chef was Carême, perhaps the greatest chef of all time. When you set out on the business of party-giving, begin with small parties and let it be known who was invited, but neglect to say who actually came. Your reputation for party-giving is created by the words of others, particularly those who are not invited but who long to come to your parties.

Discretion is an important part of the art of party-giving—never discuss what was spoken of at your party.

There is no doubt that the reputation of a person is a large part of their capacity to carry out business. In fact, the ease with which a person manages to attract deals, and the quality of the deals that a person is offered, will exactly reflect this perception. Machiavelli is quite clear on this matter. "And a Prince ought, above all things, always to endeavour in every action to gain for himself the reputation of being a great and remarkable man." He then goes on to write, "A Prince is also respected when he is either a true friend or a downright enemy. That is to say, when without reservation he declares himself in favour of one party and against the other." Today, so many people wish to take the middle way, which, of necessity, is a way that needs no courage to tread. Traversing this path will not lead to honor, nor indeed will it lead to profit either. As Machiavelli points out, this "course [committing yourself] will always be more advantageous than standing neutral: because if two of your powerful neighbours come to blows, they are of such a character that, if one of them conquers, you have either to fear him or not. In either case, it will always be more advantageous to you to declare yourself and to make war strenuously. Because, in the first case, if you do not declare yourself, you will invariably fall prey to the conqueror, to the pleasure and satisfaction of him who has been conquered, and you will have no reasons to offer, nor anything to protect or to shelter you. Because he who conquers does not count doubtful friends who will not aid him in the time of trial, and he who loses will not harbour you because you did not willingly sword in hand court his fate." The person who stays neutral and appears to risk nothing when there is everything to play for is like the stopped clock: right twice a day, but, apart from that, of little use. The one that stays neutral is a pathetic creature, winning neither the prize by taking risks, nor honor by backing what turns out to be a lost cause. Never change sides after you have supported the loser. There is honor in remaining the supporter of one who has lost and people will admire you for this honor. Those who change sides to join the winner are known for the opportunists that they are and are always treated with suspicion that in time becomes, when events are less propitious for the turncoat, contempt.

Machiavelli is quite clear on this matter: "Irresolute Princes, to avoid present dangers, generally follow the neutral path, and are generally reviled." He goes on to highlight a fact that is as completely true of business, as in most other aspects of life: "Victories, after all, are never so complete that the victor must not show some regard, especially to justice. But if he with whom you ally yourself loses, you may be sheltered by him and whilst he is able he may aid you and you become companions in a fortune that may rise again." Always remember the following piece of Machiavelli's advice: "Never let any government [or individual, for that matter] imagine that it can choose perfectly safe courses: rather let it expect to have to take very doubtful ones, because it is found in ordinary affairs that one never seeks to avoid one trouble without running into another; but prudence consists of knowing how to distinguish the character of trouble and for choice to take the lesser evil."

In truth, a proliferation of troubles, both in life and in politics, can be immensely useful, for your enemies no sooner concentrate their minds on one of your troubles, than another trouble turns up. Beware only having one trouble at a time, for all will set on you at once, beating you with that same trouble. If your troubles are many, there will be confusion over which of them your enemies should choose as a weapon to attack you. A variety of troubles lowers your threshold of fear, and new trouble coming along is as nothing by comparison to the troubles that you already have. Adding to the general confusion only increases your chances of survival.

One of the stranger aspects of life in business is that when news arrives quickly, the time scale of the consequences of that news moves into slow motion. Events take far longer to play out than could ever be imagined, even by those practiced in these matters. While the affair is drawn out, the outcome can be affected greatly by your reputation. Take care always that your reputation is for strength, courage, honor and particularly revenge.

There is a paragraph found in *The Prince* which might belong in any of that work's chapters. "Here it is noted that a Prince ought to take care never to make an alliance with one more powerful than himself, for the purpose of attacking others." This can apply to takeovers, coups in management or the manipulation of events. "Because if he conquers you are at his discretion, and Princes ought to avoid as much as possible being at the discretion of anyone."

Remember always that public relations forms the image of an employer and that image is the product of the employer's achievements, highlighted to suit the circumstances. "A Prince ought also to show himself a Patron of ability and to honour the proficient in every art, at the same time he should encourage his citizens to practise their callings peaceably, both in commerce and agriculture, and in every other following so that the one should not be deterred from improving his possessions for fear that they be taken away from him or another opening up trade for fear of taxes; but the Princes ought to offer rewards to whoever wishes to do these things and design in any way to honour his city or state." In effect, an employer must take an interest in the welfare of the company's employees and above all treat them with fairness, rewarding them for their efforts to increase the profits and so the value of the company. To do this, the employer must always remember that self-promotion is not an aim in itself and has the detrimental effect of leading the employees to believe that they who do the work are left nothing, while the employer who appears to do less takes both profit and credit. The taking of profit is acceptable, but the taking of credit which in reality is worth nothing, will cause an anger great enough, in time, to bring the whole enterprise down.

25

Why the Princes of Italy have Lost their States.

WHY BUSINESSES FAIL

For the actions of a new Prince are under far more scrutiny than those of an hereditary one. And when those actions are recognised as virtuous, they captivate men far more, and bind them to him far tighter, than ancient blood.

The person who creates a new business is a romantic figure determined to search for success and often desperate for the publicity and prestige that goes hand in hand with that success. The press eagerly search for news of these youthful tycoons and people long to read of their lifestyles. They glory in the rise of the successful tycoon and delight in the fall of the same person. To the public, such a figure is both one of envy and endless amusement. The truly successful person in business moves silently, using publicity only to advantage.

The risks taken by a person who creates a new business need not necessarily be larger than the equivalent risks taken by those whose business spans several generations. It is just that the wealth of generations, the old wealth, has far greater reserves of goodwill and reputation and therefore is able to survive where the new wealth fails. In direct proportion to the number of the generations of old wealth, so the scale of risk that each generation will be prepared to take will be reduced.

Businesses of several generations fail because they lose the desire to survive. They will not take risks, and therefore fail to make profits to refresh their reserves, while the successful new business is run by a person who does take risks and does accumulate reserves. Machiavelli continues, "Because men are attracted more by the present than the past, and when they find the present good, they enjoy it and seek to go no further." Some people are attracted by new ventures, but by far the largest group of employees would prefer to stay with an old, established firm, rather than a new company. "Thus, it will be a double glory to him to have established a new principality, and adorned and strengthened it with good laws, good areas, good allies and with good example."

A strong and decisive employer who has acted with honor and profited by this honorable conduct is an ideal but rare creature. Few have the ability to draw back from a business to seek retirement without the disturbing thoughts of unfinished work or work concluded by chicanery, leaving a sense of self-delusion. Honor is what old employers seek, and there is little honor in knowing that success has come by trickery, rather than by ability. The inheritance of a business can be a curse, changing and destroying useful lives. The irony of the amiable employer's situation was that, although he never knew, he was handed the opportunity to engage in one of the most exciting experiences given to mankind: the maintaining and improving of a business. There are no bad businesses, only badly managed businesses. The job of those who run businesses is to see into the future, to watch markets and how these markets come and go.

So, apart from bad judgment, why do businesses fail? If a business does not grow, then by definition that business fails. If a business grows too quickly, that business will also fail, for there must be a balance between the cash safely available and the cost of producing goods for sale. Markets can change far more quickly than even an optimist might imagine. A large stock on hand combined with a falling demand needs financing. Banks do not like such situations and will call in your debt regardless of how convinced you are that the market will change. It is judgment that decides between failure and success, not market demand, booms, slumps, or even war. These things can cause failure or success. It is, however, the judgment of the employer that puts the business into a position to take advantage of whatever happens. Treachery can bring failure, just as treachery can bring apparent success. However, fail or succeed with treachery and you do so without honor and without honor all is worthless. The lack of an ability to understand that events have changed will cause failure. Lightly entering into guarantees and liabilities will bring about failure, as will being deserted by your followers and supporters. Indeed, being restrained from taking crucial actions by colleagues at a time when these actions need to be taken can lead to failure. The cause of this failure is not your colleagues, rather your own lack of will.

The moment to beware of expansion is when times are good. Overexpansion just before a recession brings failure. Similarly, to acquire a burden of debt is dangerous at the beginning of a recession. Careful expansion in a recession is never harmful. Debt must sometimes be taken on; but equally, debt must be given a priority when funds become available and to neglect to do this leads to failure. Extravagance often leads to failure and extravagance is found in many firms, for those who run businesses are often blind to their own extravagances. Fraud is sometimes so cunning that even the most astute people cannot spot it. Fraud is exposed by failure, but seldom causes that failure, for a clever thief keeps the victim alive so that robbery can be practiced again.

None of these reasons will kill a business when times are good. Any one of them will kill a business when times are bad. In good times, each of these problems can be addressed and resolved; in bad times, there are neither the resources available, nor the goodwill of those around you to deal with issues such as these. In bad times, both the people who conduct businesses and the practices that they use become hardened. These adverse circumstances justify in the minds of many the need to be unnecessarily hard. "Therefore, do not let our Princes accuse fortune for the loss of their Principalities after so many years possession, but rather their own sloth. Because in quiet times they never thought there could be change. And when, afterwards, the bad times come, they thought of flight and not of defending themselves, and they hoped that the people disgusted with the insolence of the conquerors would recall them." The conquerors stayed and in time the people loved their conquerors about as much as they had loved the amiable employer, which in truth was not at all. People respect competence, and there is no greater way to demonstrate competence than to win. Winning gives so much more strength to your promises than losing.

No person can truly win on their own. The road to success is hard and full of pitfalls and is better traveled in company. Two heads are better than one, as has been proven time and time again in business. It is far better to have a partner to pull you from the pit when you stumble and for you to do likewise for your partner. If a partner is not readily available, or acceptable, then choose a colleague. These two minds, while being of the same philosophy, must have different talents, talents complementary to one another.

Never, in all your trials and tribulations—for rest assured they will be many—refuse help, and what is more important, take that help gracefully when it is offered. Always, however, be scrupulous in repaying such help as you receive or are offered. Remember Machiavelli's words when you search for solutions to the problem of achieving success: "Those [solutions] only are reliable, certain and durable that depend on yourself and your valour."

26

How Much Fortune can Influence Human Affairs, and How She Should be Resisted.

CREATING ONE'S OWN LUCK

I am not unaware that many were, and still are of the opinion that human affairs are so governed by fortune and God that man is incapable of managing them with his prudence, indeed, that man has no remedy at all. They would therefore judge it worthless to sweat unduly over things, letting themselves be governed by chance.

It is true that chance seems to play a great part in the affairs of mankind. However, it is important to know that skill can overcome chance. In the game of backgammon, players throw the same dice from the same cup. One player is in the hands of luck and sometimes luck favors that player, letting the dice fall at the right numbers to suit the deployment of that player's counters. At another time, luck does not favor that player, the dice never seeming to produce numbers that are in any way helpful. This player is totally in the hands of luck. The player's opponent, who relies not on luck, but rather on mathematics, has the counters so arranged that whatever number is shown by the dice is useful. The opponent has calculated the variations of numbers produced by two dice falling from a cup. One player takes advantage of luck, the other player makes luck. Machiavelli would take a middle course. "I hold it to be true that Fortune is the arbiter of one half of our actions." Frederick the Great, however, was of the view that the older one gets the more convinced one becomes that His Majesty King Chance does three quarters of the business of this miserable Universe.

Neither statement is true. The actions that people take, however carefully considered, sometimes go wrong. As a result, failure is put down to ill luck. But is this really justified? Fate may intervene as an event that could not be foreseen and is more often than not given a helping hand by a perfectly understandable oversight. Luck is when the unforeseen works in our favor. Ill luck is when the unforeseen works against us. So luck is not magic, but simply a lacuna in our knowledge that works for us or against us. Luck is a remarkably fine excuse to justify failure. In the words of Oscar Wilde: "Success is entirely due to luck." To confirm this view he suggested asking anyone who has failed.

Machiavelli writes well of fortune and his words of five hundred years ago are as true today as they were true then. "I compare her [luck] to one of those raging rivers which when in flood overflows the plains, sweeping away trees and buildings, bearing away soil from place to place; everything flies before it, all yield to its violence without being able in any way to withstand it; and yet though its nature be such, it does not follow therefore that men, when the weather becomes fair, shall not make provision both with defences and barriers, in such manner that, rising again, the waters may pass away and their force be neither unrestrained nor so dangerous. So it happens with Fortune, who shows her power where valour has not prepared to resist her, and thither she turns her forces where she knows that barriers and defences have not been raised to constrain her."

What we call luck favors those who prepare the way for luck, and similarly, those who seem to have bad luck continue to have bad luck, for they are making a mistake in how they set about their business. They cannot see that mistake, either through a blindness brought about by lack of ability and compounded by habit, or just stubbornness. All this is obscured by that convenient excuse: "ill luck." Furthermore, Machiavelli writes, "The Prince who relies entirely on fortune is lost when it changes. I believe also that he will be successful who directs his actions according to the spirit of the times, and he whose actions do not accord with his times will not be successful, because men are seen in affairs that lead to the end which every man has before him, namely glory and riches, to get there by various methods."

There are well-defined cycles in business activity. Where these cycles will start and where they will end is, however, uncertain and a matter of judgment. No boom is sustainable because, by definition, if there is no dip then that boom becomes a state of affairs. People and businesses adapt to that state of affairs and the beneficial effects of a boom are lost. Booms and the resultant dips are both beneficial, for they change the social order of a country in a way that a tide cleans the beach. Recessions which last far longer than dips are unsatisfactory, for they benefit no one. However, recessions are not permanent, for governments finding that recessions and unpopularity go hand in hand, eventually set about changing the state of affairs that cause them. A level state of affairs benefits only the timid and the idle. The poor stay poor, the rich stay rich. High interest rates have the same effect. Because of high interest rates and because those benefiting from such a level state of affairs are the ones less able to produce prosperity, matters will in time change. The electorate begins to observe the disadvantages of a level state of affairs and will become increasingly displeased with those who govern it. To spot that change is called "luck" by some, and by others "timing."

The sensitivity to spot a change in the order of events is one of the richest gifts given to mankind, a gift that is given sparingly. If a person spots a change that other people cannot detect and then changes his or her own manner and style, that person is ahead of others. However, this position will do that person little good, for others will mock the folly of actions that set that person apart. To be in the advance of the thought of others is gratifying, but seldom rewarding. A person who would succeed must catch the first swelling of the wave of thought and then ride that wave like one who rides on the ocean surf. Remember, however, that the waves of opinion come and go, and the evidence that changes the ocean's flat surface into a rolling wave of opinion does not have to be true evidence. Waves of opinion are created quite as frequently by false evidence as they are by the truth. The wave you ride will break into surf on the mainland shore and in the end will be a pathetic ripple only moving grains of sand. Behind the great waves that you will ride will come another as great or even greater, and if you will succeed then you must be able to move with mental agility from one wave of opinion before it breaks, to another wave of opinion, before it peaks. Such a one will be deemed to be "blessed by luck."

Machiavelli observes that in hard times it is not just the cautious who survive, nor in good times just the impetuous who prosper. Machiavelli concludes that: "All this arises from nothing else than whether or not they conform in the methods to the spirit of the times." To be in tune with your times is vitally important if you hope to succeed, not only in business but also in any other walk of life.

People who cannot change are in the hands of luck; people adept at change make their own luck. "He is ruined if he does not change his course of action. But a man is not often found sufficiently circumspect to know how to accommodate himself to the change. Both because he cannot deviate from what nature inclines him to, and also because having always prospered by acting in one way, he cannot be persuaded that it is well to leave it. And, therefore, the cautious man, when it is time to turn adventurous, does not know how to do it hence he is ruined. But had he changed, his conduct with the times fortune would not have been changed." There has seldom been a better piece of advice given to those who would prosper in business, though changing your style to be in tune with the times is not the only method of giving your "luck" a nudge.

A sharp change in style will always wrong-foot an opponent, be the opponent either within or without your company. The battle of wills must be fought to a rhythm. The Russian army was a master of this tactic invented in the nineteenth century by General Barclay de Tolly. Attack, retreat, appear to attack, appear to retreat, wrong-foot your enemy and then destroy that enemy and let mankind call your success luck. Remember always that the person who is unexpectedly rash in their attack also makes their luck, as did Pope Julius II. "Therefore Julius with his impetuous action accomplished what no other pontiff with simple wisdom could have done; for if he had waited in Rome until he could get away, with his plans arranged and everything fixed, as any other pontiff would have done, he would never have succeeded, because the King of France would have made a thousand excuses, and the others would have raised a thousand fears." Instead Pope Julius made an unexpected attack on the city of Bologna and took it. The unexpected, the ambush, is often more successful than people believe.

Intentions, good or bad, are capable of change, as we all know. When preparing for the unexpected, it is not the intention of the enemy that needs to be taken into account, rather the enemy's capacity to attack you. Capacity is the physical capability to bring something to fruition. It can be watched and monitored, and is therefore the only really trustworthy guide to danger. With ambush and the unexpected attack, or even treachery, people drive their luck. However, when that luck runs out, when those greater than they decide to put a stop to these tricks, then those people who drive their luck must distance themselves from events, and consider the mistakes that they have made. Only in that way will they discover that the apparent change in their luck is due to a change in circumstance, making it no longer propitious to behave as they once behaved.

What constitutes luck in business—an unexpected contract, or sale, a meeting in a public place that leads to a profitable deal, finding that a person whom you once helped is now in a position to help you? Remember that the circles that you move in socially are intersected by the circles that you move in during your business life. Both of these two sets of circles are again intersected by a series of other circles, from your education to the sports that you play, the clubs that you join, the town that you live in. It is not chance that you meet the person who can help you at a particular moment, for it is likely that you (whether you realize it or not) know where to find that person at a time when you need to meet them.

Machiavelli sums the matter up thus, "For my part I consider that it is better to be adventurous than cautious, because fortune is a woman, and if you wish to keep her under, it is necessary to beat and ill-use her; and it is seen that she allows herself to be mastered by the adventurous rather than by those who go to work more coldly. She is, therefore, always woman like, a lover of young men, because they are less cautious, more violent and with more audacity, command her."

Machiavelli would find the last years of the twentieth century a strange world, for much has changed since the fifteenth century, not least the attitude of women towards men who would beat them. Machiavelli would have to adapt much of what he wrote to the modern age, as I have tried to adapt his writings. However, the thrust of Machiavelli's words are still relevant today, still at the heart of the advice which should be given to the one who would prosper in business. Courage, honor, energy, ability, perseverance and, above all, total dedication are the ingredients of success. As for luck, approach both luck and God with caution. The former is, even with the best of efforts, uncertain, while the latter demonstrates quite regularly the certainty only of death.

In the end, whether or not your business prospers or fails is all a matter of how you behave and the decisions that you take. It is up to you. The secret of success, if there is such a simple and singular secret, is the determination to succeed and not the determination to avoid failure.